PASSOVER
THE HEALTHY WAY

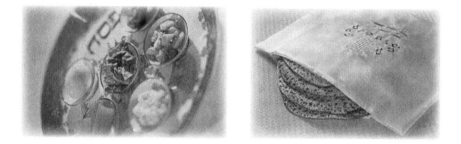

Light, Tasty and *Easy* Recipes
Your Whole Family Will Enjoy

BONNIE R. GILLER, MS, RD, CDN, CDE
REGISTERED DIETITIAN

authorHOUSE®

AuthorHouse™
1663 Liberty Drive
Bloomington, IN 47403
www.authorhouse.com
Phone: 1-800-839-8640

First published by AuthorHouse 03/18/2011

ISBN: 978-1-4490-7940-6 (sc)
ISBN: 978-1-4490-7941-3 (e)

Library of Congress Control Number: 2010901487

Printed in the United States of America
Bloomington, Indiana

This book is printed on acid-free paper.

To my husband, Michael, and children, Matthew and Shaina, Jason, Jennifer and Lauren – for your constant support and patience; and my parents, Ruth and Danny Berger, for all your guidance, encouragement and love.

CONTENTS

ACKNOWLEDGMENTS

I have many people to thank for their support in the completion of this cookbook. First, I'd like to express my sincere appreciation to my family and friends who shared their favorite Passover recipes and were open to my suggestions for modifications. All recipes were analyzed and modified to provide delicious dishes that are low in fat and calories.

Thank you to my many "recipe testers and tasters". To my mother Ruth Berger, mother-in-law Bina Giller, sister-in-law Amy, Eleni, Lisa and Laura - your willingness to spend time in the kitchen has helped bring this cookbook to fruition. A very special thank you to my daughter, Jennifer, who stood side-by-side with me in the kitchen testing recipes. Not only are you "quick", but you also clean up the "mess" you make. I look forward to having you as my partner in many more projects.

To my fantastic assistants, Eleni, Lisa and Laura – thank you for your speedy word processing and proofreading skills. Eleni, your dedication to helping me complete this project in a timely fashion is very much appreciated.

And of course, thank you to my most "critical" taste testers - my husband and children. You often commented that it "tastes like Passover in December" but you were willing participants and gave me your honest opinions. Thank you for your encouragement, excitement, advice and support in this, and in all the projects that I undertake.

ABOUT THE AUTHOR

Bonnie R. Giller is a Registered Dietitian (R.D.) and is certified by the New York State Education Department as a Certified Dietitian-Nutritionist (CDN). Bonnie operates a successful private practice in beautiful Long Island, New York. Since 1987, Bonnie has helped thousands of individuals achieve their nutrition and fitness goals. Bonnie is committed to improving the health of individuals through positive lifestyle changes and healthier eating habits.

As a registered and certified dietitian-nutritionist, Bonnie provides Medical Nutrition Therapy for weight management and many medical conditions to adults and children of all ages. Bonnie is also a Certified Diabetes Educator (C.D.E.) assisting those with diabetes to understand their complex medical condition, stabilize their blood glucose levels and learn proper meal planning techniques. Bonnie is certified in Family & Consumer Sciences, with her focus being nutrition education for the entire family.

Bonnie specializes in the following areas of medical nutrition therapy:

+ Diabetes, including type 1, type 2, and gestational

+ Insulin resistance

+ Cardiovascular disease, including high cholesterol, high triglycerides and hypertension

✦ Gastrointestinal conditions, including IBS, Crohn's Disease, Ulcerative Colitis, Diverticulosis/Diverticulitis, Reflux Disease, Lactose Intolerance

✦ Weight Management (loss or gain)

Previously, Bonnie was the director of an American Dietetic Association accredited dietetic internship program in the New York Metropolitan area, run by the largest contract management company in North America. In this role, Bonnie taught and coordinated the learning experience of dietetic interns. Bonnie was also the Clinical Nutrition Manager at Jamaica Hospital Medical Center, a large teaching facility in Queens, New York.

Bonnie enjoys giving lectures to both the professional and lay audience. Topics presented include Demystifying Common Nutrition Myths, Nutritious Treats for the Entire Family, Putting the Pyramid into Practice, Nutrition and Osteoporosis, Nutrition and Aging, and Nutrition Education in the Preschool Years.

Bonnie is the author of *Recipes to Remember: Heart Healthy Can Be Delicious*, a cookbook with 200 recipes that your heart will love. In addition, her first Passover cookbook titled *Matzoh & More: Tasty and Delicious Passover Recipes* is a unique collection of twenty of her favorite Passover recipes.

Bonnie earned her Bachelor of Arts degree in Food and Nutrition from Queens College in Flushing, New York and her Master of Science degree in Clinical Nutrition from Brooklyn College in Brooklyn, New York. She completed her dietetic internship at North Shore University Hospital (formerly Central General Hospital) in Plainview, New York. She is a member of many professional associations.

Services Available at BRG Dietetics & Nutrition, P.C.

* Individual Nutrition Counseling

* Group/Family Nutrition Counseling

* Menu Development

* Computerized Menu and Recipe Analysis

516-486-4569
www.brghealth.com

INTRODUCTION

I set out to write this Passover cookbook because of four common concerns that I hear year after year from my clients. The first concern: "I never get out of the kitchen; I am constantly cooking and baking." Second, "I always gain weight over Passover." Third, "every Passover recipe contains huge amounts of eggs and oil" and fourth, "I serve the same recipes with little variety each year."

With proper planning and recipe modification, your Passover recipes can be low in fat and healthy. If you're wondering if there is anything to serve besides meat and potatoes that is *also* healthy and tasty, you'll find your answer in this cookbook *Passover the Healthy Way*. Delicious recipes ranging from Matzoh Stuffed Chicken Cutlets to a delicious Pineapple-Cherry Ribbon will banish boredom and unhealthy dishes from your Passover menus. These healthy and creative recipes will help you breeze through Passover without sacrificing taste and originality. With proper portion control, you will be able to maintain your weight over the holiday, get out of the kitchen to enjoy your company, and be greeted at the dinner table with cheers and excitement.

This handy cookbook is great for the Passover traveler or the stay-at-home, traditional holiday crowd. Enjoy!

About the Recipes

The recipes in this cookbook have been designed to reduce your intake of calories, fat, saturated fat, cholesterol and sodium. Some recipes have been modified by reducing the amount of the ingredient, by substituting a preferred ingredient or by eliminating the ingredient. Common substitutions include using unsweetened applesauce for some of the oil originally called for in a recipe, using less sugar, and/or replacing whole eggs with egg whites or egg substitute.

Sodium

The American Heart Association and the American Diabetes Association recommend a sodium intake of no more than 1500 mg per day. Those on a sodium-restricted meal plan most commonly limit their sodium to no more than 1500-2000 mg per day. To put this in perspective, one teaspoon of table salt contains 2300 mg of sodium. Thus, the recommendation for those on a sodium restriction is to avoid cooking with salt and adding salt to their food at the table.

Low sodium chicken or vegetable broth was used in the recipes when possible. Salt is used in some of the recipes, however, those on a sodium restriction should eliminate the salt. The sodium content of the recipe will then be reduced.

Sugar

Use of sugar in the recipes has been kept to a minimum where possible. However, sugar must be used in some recipes, for example, in baked goods and cake recipes. A cake cannot hold its shape without the addition of sugar. While sugar substitutes are available for Passover, the final product of the baked goods did not come out acceptable. In addition, several artificial sweeteners lose its sweetness when exposed to heat and some acquire a bitter aftertaste if exposed to high temperatures for a long time. I therefore decided to use sugar, but I decreased the amount called for in the original recipe.

Whether you are watching your weight, counting your calories, or you have diabetes, baked goods should be eaten in moderation and only on occasion. If your blood sugar level is elevated, you should avoid these foods until your levels are better controlled.

Exchange Lists

Exchange lists or food groups are commonly used in many weight loss plans and in diabetes meal planning. The exchange lists provide you with a variety of common foods to select from to meet your individual preferences. Foods are divided into six lists based on their nutritive composition of carbohydrate, protein and fat. Each serving of food has the same amount of carbohydrate, protein, fat and calories as the other foods on that list. That is why any food on the list can be "exchanged" or traded for any other food on the list. It is incorrect to exchange food items between lists, since the nutritional value is different.

Each recipe in this cookbook has the *Exchanges per Serving* listed. The figures used to calculate the exchanges are based on the American Dietetic Association and American Diabetes Association Exchange Lists for Meal Planning. It is important to note that the calories, carbohydrate, protein and fat assigned to each exchange list are averages and not always the exact values for a specific food within that exchange list. The calories listed for each recipe are within 20 calories of the combined caloric value of the exchanges listed for each recipe. Exchanges were rounded to the nearest ½ to make it easier for those who are following an exchange list meal plan. For example, if a serving of stuffing equals 1 1/3 of a starch serving, the final exchange is listed as 1 ½ starch servings.

Nutritional Analysis

The nutritional analysis that appears with each recipe was done using a professional nutritional analysis software program. However, because numerous variables account for a wide range of values for certain foods, nutritional analyses should be considered approximate. Values for total fat, saturated fat, polyunsaturated and monounsaturated fat were rounded according to the FDA rounding rules. Thus, it is possible that the total fat value does not always equal the sum of the fatty acids listed.

The analysis of each recipe includes all the ingredients listed for a recipe except ingredients that are listed as *"optional"* or *"for garnish"*. If an ingredient is listed as *"a dash of"* or *"to taste"*, the value used in the calculation was 1/8 teaspoon.

"Prepared" Matzoh

Some of the recipes state in the ingredient list to use "prepared" matzoh. This is matzoh that you have soaked and softened in advance for use in the recipes.

The following process can be used to "prepare" the matzoh. Wet both sides of a sheet of paper towel. Place the wet paper towel onto the counter. Run one piece of matzoh under cool tap water, wetting both sides. Place on top of the wet paper towel. Continue this layering process until you finish one box of matzoh. Check every 15 minutes until the matzoh obtains an al-dente feel. Unlayer the matzoh and let dry, about 10 minutes. Store in a storage bag in the refrigerator.

Note: The recipes in this cookbook are kosher and are meant to be prepared using kosher ingredients. Consult with your local Rabbi when necessary.

Soups & Salads

SOUPS & SALADS

Broccoli and Carrot Vinaigrette

Serves: 6

1 lb. fresh broccoli flowerets
2 carrots, sliced
2 tbsp. olive oil
¼ cup cider or wine vinegar
½ tsp. paprika
1 tbsp. chopped chives (optional)
1 tsp. dried parsley flakes, or 1 tbsp. chopped fresh
1 clove garlic, minced
Salt and pepper to taste

1. Steam broccoli and carrots until crisp tender; allow to cool.
2. Whisk or beat together the remaining ingredients.
3. Combine and chill.
4. Toss and serve cold.

Serving Size: ½ cup
Exchanges per Serving: 1 Vegetable, 1 Fat

Nutrition Facts

Calories: 76
Total Fat: 5 gm
Saturated Fat: 1 gm
Polyunsaturated Fat: 0.5 gm
Monounsaturated Fat: 3.5 gm

Cholesterol: 0 mg
Protein: 3 gm
Carbohydrate: 7 gm
Dietary Fiber: 1 gm
Sodium: 424 mg

Carrot Soup

Serves: 6

8 medium carrots, peeled and sliced
4 onions, sliced
1 tsp. oil
6 cups low sodium vegetable broth
1/3 cup parsley, chopped
Pepper to taste

1. In a three quart pot, sauté the onions and carrots until soft.
2. Add vegetable broth, seasonings, and parsley. Bring to a boil, reduce heat and cover. Simmer for 45 minutes.
3. Puree using an immersion blender until thick.

Serving Size: 1 cup
Exchanges per Serving: 2 Vegetable

□□□□□□□□□□□□□□□□□□□□

Nutrition Facts

Calories: 99
Total Fat: 1 gm
Saturated Fat: 0 gm
Polyunsaturated Fat: 0.5 gm
Monounsaturated Fat: 0 gm

Cholesterol: 0 mg
Protein: 2 gm
Carbohydrate: 21 gm
Dietary Fiber: 5 gm
Sodium: 201 mg

□□□□□□□□□□□□□□□□□□□□

Citus Carrot Salad

Serves: 12

8 medium carrots, peeled and grated
2 naval oranges, peeled, sectioned, and chopped
Juice of half a lemon
1 tbsp. dried mint, or 3 tbsp. fresh
1/3 cup raisins
1 tsp. grated orange zest

1. Toss all ingredients together in a large bowl.
2. Chill before serving.

Serving Size: ½ cup
Exchanges per Serving: 1 Vegetable, ½ Fruit

Nutrition Facts

Calories: 40
Total Fat: 0 gm
Saturated Fat: 0 gm
Polyunsaturated Fat: 0 gm
Monounsaturated Fat: 0 gm

Cholesterol: 0 mg
Protein: 1 gm
Carbohydrate: 10 gm
Dietary Fiber: 2 gm
Sodium: 29 mg

Eggplant Salad

Serves: 6

1 medium eggplant
1 medium onion, chopped
1 medium green pepper, chopped
1 garlic clove
Pinch of salt & pepper

1. Broil eggplant on flame until very soft. Remove charred skin and mash the eggplant.
2. Add chopped onion and green pepper to mashed eggplant.
3. Add garlic clove, using garlic press.
4. Season with salt and pepper.
5. Mix well and serve on lettuce leaf. Garnish with parsley.

Serving Size: ½ cup
Exchanges per Serving: 1 ½ Vegetable

Nutrition Facts

Calories: 37
Total Fat: 0 gm
Saturated Fat: 0 gm
Polyunsaturated Fat: 0 gm
Monounsaturated Fat: 0 gm

Cholesterol: 0 mg
Protein: 1 gm
Carbohydrate: 9 gm
Dietary Fiber: 4 gm
Sodium: 52 mg

Herbed Matzoh Balls

Serves: 12

2 whole eggs
6 tbsp. seltzer
¼ cup oil
Salt and pepper to taste
1 cup matzoh meal
2 tbsp. finely chopped fresh mint
2 tbsp. finely chopped fresh dill
1 tsp. ground ginger powder
4 egg whites

1. Mix eggs, seltzer, oil, salt and pepper.
2. Stir in matzoh meal and herbs.
3. Beat egg whites until stiff peaks form. Fold into matzoh meal mixture.
4. Refrigerate for 2 hours. With wet hands, shape matzoh balls.
5. Add to boiling water. Simmer matzoh balls for about 28-30 minutes.

Serving Size: 1 matzoh ball
Exchanges per Serving: ½ Starch, 1 Fat

Nutrition Facts

Calories: 96
Total Fat: 5 gm
Saturated Fat: 0.5 gm
Polyunsaturated Fat: 3.5 gm
Monounsaturated Fat: 1 gm

Cholesterol: 35 mg
Protein: 3 gm
Carbohydrate: 8 gm
Dietary Fiber: 0 gm
Sodium: 225 mg

Lemon Dressed Carrots

Serves: 8

5 cups (½ inch thick) carrot slices (~10 medium carrots)
2 garlic cloves, halved
2/3 cup fresh lemon juice
¼ cup chopped fresh parsley
2 tbsp. sweetener
1 tsp. ground cinnamon
½ tsp. ground cumin
½ tsp. paprika

1. Steam carrots and garlic until tender; drain. Discard garlic.
2. Combine lemon juice and remaining ingredients in a medium bowl; stir well.
3. Add lemon juice mixture to carrots, toss to coat.
4. Serve at either room temperature or chilled.

Serving Size: ½ cup
Exchanges per Serving: 2 Vegetable

Nutrition Facts

Calories: 40
Total Fat: 0 gm
Saturated Fat: 0 gm
Polyunsaturated Fat: 0 gm
Monounsaturated Fat: 0 gm

Cholesterol: 0 mg
Protein: 1 gm
Carbohydrate: 10 gm
Dietary Fiber: 2 gm
Sodium: 55 mg

Potato Leek Soup

Serves: 4

5 cups leeks, trimmed and sliced
2 ½ cups red potatoes, peeled and cubed
4 cups fat-free, low sodium chicken broth
1 tbsp. scallions, chopped for garnish

1. Combine all ingredients except scallions in a large pot and bring to a boil. Lower the heat, cover and simmer for 1 hour.
2. Transfer to a food processor or use an immersion blender to puree the soup.
3. Return the soup to the pot and reheat for 3 minutes.
4. Garnish with the chopped scallions and serve.

Serving Size: 1 cup
Exchanges per Serving: 1 Starch, 3 Vegetable

□□□□□□□□□□□□□□□□□□□□□

Nutrition Facts

Calories: 151
Total Fat: 0 gm
Saturated Fat: 0 gm
Polyunsaturated Fat: 0 gm
Monounsaturated Fat: 0 gm

Cholesterol: 0 mg
Protein: 6 gm
Carbohydrate: 32 gm
Dietary Fiber: 3 gm
Sodium: 88 mg

□□□□□□□□□□□□□□□□□□□□□

Tomato and Pepper Salad

Serves: 8

2 cups diced tomato
1 cup diced green pepper
1 cup diced yellow pepper
1 cup diced onion
¼ cup chopped parsley
¼ cup fresh lemon juice
2 tsp. olive oil
¼ tsp. salt
¼ tsp. pepper

1. Combine tomato, green and yellow pepper, and onion in a bowl.
2. In a separate bowl, mix lemon juice, olive oil, and parsley. Season with salt and pepper.
3. Mix dressing with tomato and pepper mixture. Toss until well-coated.
4. Chill for several hours or overnight.

Serving Size: ½ cup
Exchanges per Serving: 1 ½ Vegetable

Nutrition Facts

Calories: 38
Total Fat: 1.5 gm
Saturated Fat: 0 gm
Polyunsaturated Fat: 0 gm
Monounsaturated Fat: 1 gm

Cholesterol: 0 mg
Protein: 1 gm
Carbohydrate: 6 gm
Dietary Fiber: 1 gm
Sodium: 78 mg

Traditional Matzoh Balls

Serves: 12

2 eggs, separated
4 egg whites
½ cup water
1/3 cup olive oil
1 tsp. salt
¼ tsp. black pepper
1 cup matzoh meal

1. In a small bowl, beat egg whites until foamy.
2. In a second bowl, beat egg yolks, water, oil, salt and pepper.
3. Fold in egg whites, then fold in matzoh meal. Chill for 1 hour.
4. Form into balls; boil in 1 ½ quarts of water for 20 minutes, uncovered.

Serving Size: 1 matzoh ball
Exchanges per Serving: 1 Starch, 1 ½ Fat

Nutrition Facts

Calories: 113
Total Fat: 7 gm
Saturated Fat: 1 gm
Polyunsaturated Fat: 1 gm
Monounsaturated Fat: 5 gm

Cholesterol: 35 mg
Protein: 3 gm
Carbohydrate: 10 gm
Dietary Fiber: 0 gm
Sodium: 225 mg

Turnip and Leek Soup

Serves: 5

3 stalks celery, sliced
1 leek, cleaned, trimmed, and sliced (white and green parts only)
1 carrot, peeled and chopped
1 turnip, peeled and chopped
¼ cabbage, chopped
1 medium potato, peeled and cubed
5 cups low sodium chicken broth
1 tbsp. fresh cilantro or parsley

1. In a large heavy pot, combine all the ingredients except the cilantro. Bring to a boil, reduce heat, and simmer until all of the vegetables are tender, about 20-30 minutes.
2. Stir in the cilantro or parsley. Remove from heat. Using an immersion blender, blend soup until smooth.

Serving Size: 1 cup
Exchanges per Serving: 1 ½ Vegetable, ½ Starch

Nutrition Facts

Calories: 77
Total Fat: 0 gm
Saturated Fat: 0 gm
Polyunsaturated Fat: 0 gm
Monounsaturated Fat: 0 gm

Cholesterol: 0 mg
Protein: 4 gm
Carbohydrate: 15 gm
Dietary Fiber: 3 gm
Sodium: 117 mg

Vegetable Soup

Serves: 5

1 tsp. olive oil
½ cup onion, chopped
½ cup celery, diced
2 garlic cloves
1 ½ cups no salt added tomato juice
1 ¼ cups low sodium vegetable broth
1 cup carrots
1/8 tsp. black pepper
2 cups zucchini, sliced
1 cup tomato, diced
1 tsp. parsley, chopped

1. Sauté onion, celery and garlic in olive oil until softened.
2. Add remaining ingredients and bring to a boil.
3. Reduce heat to low, cover and simmer until carrots are tender, approximately 30-40 minutes.
4. Remove from heat. Using an immersion blender, blend until smooth.

Serving Size: 1 cup
Exchanges per Serving: 2 Vegetables

Nutrition Facts

Calories: 58
Total Fat: 1 gm
Saturated Fat: 0 gm
Polyunsaturated Fat: 0 gm
Monounsaturated Fat: 1 gm

Cholesterol: 0 mg
Protein: 2 gm
Carbohydrate: 11 gm
Dietary Fiber: 3 gm
Sodium: 75 mg

Zesty Chicken Soup

Serves: 10

1 large chicken, cut into pieces, no skin
3 quarts cold water
2 medium onions, quartered
2 carrots, julienned
2 stalks celery, julienned
2 medium zucchini, julienned
Pinch of white pepper
½ cup chopped fresh parsley
¼ cup fresh dill
½ tbsp. lemon zest
½ tbsp. ginger root, grated

1. Place chicken in a large soup pot.
2. Add cold water and bring close to a boil. Add remaining ingredients, except fresh herbs.
3. Cover and simmer for 1 ½ hours or until chicken is tender. Add fresh herbs and cook for another 10 minutes.
4. Place in refrigerator overnight. The next day, skim fat from the top.
5. Heat and serve.

Serving Size: 1 cup
Exchanges per Serving: 2 Meat, 1 Vegetable

Nutrition Facts

Calories: 106
Total Fat: 2 gm
Saturated Fat: 0.5 gm
Monounsaturated Fat: 0.5 gm
Polyunsaturated Fat: 0.5 gm

Cholesterol: 46 mg
Protein: 15 gm
Carbohydrate: 6 gm
Dietary Fiber: 2 gm
Sodium: 81 mg

NOTE: You can use fresh mint, cilantro or any other herbs for a different taste.

Poultry & Other Meats

POULTRY &
OTHER MEATS

Apricot Chicken

Serves: 4

4 (4 oz. each) chicken quarters, no skin
4 tbsp. reduced or sugar-free apricot jam
½ packet low sodium onion soup mix
1 tsp. lemon juice
1/3 cup fat free Italian dressing

1. Mix all the ingredients and marinate the chicken in the refrigerator overnight or for several hours.
2. Bake for 1 hour at 350 degrees F.

Serving Size: 1 chicken quarter
Exchanges per Serving: 3 Meat

Nutrition Facts

Calories: 171
Total Fat: 3.5 gm
Saturated Fat: 1 gm
Polyunsaturated Fat: 1 gm
Monounsaturated Fat: 1 gm

Cholesterol: 80 mg
Protein: 25 gm
Carbohydrate: 10 gm
Dietary Fiber: 0 gm
Sodium: 526 mg

Cabbage Apple Chicken

Serves: 4

4 boneless, skinless chicken breasts (~ 1 lb.)
¼ tsp. freshly ground pepper
1 tbsp. lemon juice
1 tbsp. dry white wine
1 tsp. olive oil
8 oz. package of coleslaw mix
1 apple, sliced
1 tsp. sugar
½ tsp. cider vinegar

1. Preheat oven to 350 degrees F.
2. Coat a Pyrex baking dish with non-stick cooking spray. Arrange chicken breasts in the pan; sprinkle with pepper, then drizzle with lemon juice and wine.
3. Cover tightly and bake until chicken is white all the way through and juices run clear, 20 to 25 minutes.
4. While chicken bakes, heat olive oil in a separate skillet over medium-high heat; add coleslaw mix, sliced apple, sugar, and cider vinegar.
5. Cook until vegetables are tender, about 10 minutes.
6. When chicken is cooked, remove from oven and add topping.

Serving Size: 1 chicken breast with ¼ of the topping
Exchanges per Serving: 3 Meat, ½ Vegetable

Nutrition Facts

Calories: 178
Total Fat: 2.5 gm
Saturated Fat: 0.5 gm
Polyunsaturated Fat: 0.5 gm
Monounsaturated Fat: 1 gm

Cholesterol: 66 mg
Protein: 27 gm
Carbohydrate: 10 gm
Dietary Fiber: 2 gm
Sodium: 91 mg

Chicken with Honey-Wine Sauce

Serves: 8

2 whole chickens, cut into quarters (~1 ½ lbs. each)
½ tsp. pepper
1 cup dry red wine
3 garlic cloves, crushed
1 tsp. dried thyme
1 tsp. dried basil
1 tsp. dried sage
¼ cup honey

1. Preheat oven to 400 degrees F.
2. Place chicken in a large, deep roasting pan.
3. Sprinkle with pepper.
4. Combine remaining ingredients, stirring to dissolve honey.
5. Pour over chicken.
6. Roast, basting frequently, until chicken is tender and browned, about 1 ¼-1 ½ hours.

Serving Size: 1 chicken quarter
Exchanges per Serving: 5 Meat, ½ Fruit

Nutrition Facts

Calories: 255
Total fat: 5 gm
Saturated Fat: 1.5 gm
Polyunsaturated Fat: 1 gm
Monounsaturated Fat: 1.5 gm

Cholesterol: 115 mg
Protein: 35 gm
Carbohydrate: 10 gm
Dietary Fiber: 0 gm
Sodium: 129 mg

Confetti Turkey Loaf

Serves: 5

1 lb. ground white meat turkey
2 egg whites
¼ cup matzoh meal
2 tbsp. chopped onion
2 tbsp. chopped red pepper
2 tbsp. chopped green pepper
4 tbsp. salsa, divided
1/8 tsp. black pepper
1 tsp. mustard
¼ cup water

1. Combine all ingredients except 2 tbsp. salsa. Mix well. Press into 5 ½ x 9½ inch loaf pan.
2. Brush top of loaf with remaining salsa and bake in 350 degree F oven for 1 hour 15 minutes or until meat is no longer pink in center.

Serving Size: 1 slice
Exchanges per Serving: 3 Meat

Nutrition Facts

Calories: 139
Total Fat: 1.5 gm
Saturated Fat: 0.5 gm
Polyunsaturated Fat: 0 gm
Monounsaturated Fat: 0 gm

Cholesterol: 54 mg
Protein: 24 gm
Carbohydrate: 6 gm
Dietary Fiber: 0.5 gm
Sodium: 144 mg

Grilled Orange Chicken Salad

Serves: 8

Salad:
2 lbs. boneless chicken breasts, raw
11 oz. Mandarin oranges, drained
8 cups romaine lettuce, shredded
½ cup green pepper, chopped
½ cup red pepper, chopped
½ cup cucumber, chopped
1 medium tomato, sliced

Dressing:
½ cup orange juice
2 tbsp. oil
1 ½ tbsp. sugar
½ cup white wine vinegar
¼ tbsp. garlic & herb seasoning

1. Whisk together all dressing ingredients. Set aside ½ cup. Brush chicken with reserved dressing.
2. Grill chicken, turning and brushing occasionally until done. Cut chicken into strips.
3. Toss romaine lettuce with Mandarin oranges, peppers, cucumbers, and tomato. Top with grilled chicken strips and drizzle with remaining dressing.

Serving Size: 4 oz. grilled chicken atop 1 cup greens with oranges, vegetables, and 1 tbsp. dressing
Exchanges per Serving: 4 Meat, 1 Vegetable, 1 Fat

□□□□□□□□□□□□□□□□□□□□

Nutrition Facts

Calories: 217
Total Fat: 5 gm
Saturated Fat: 0.5 gm
Polyunsaturated Fat: 3 gm
Monounsaturated Fat: 1 gm

Cholesterol: 66 mg
Protein: 27 gm
Carbohydrate: 13 gm
Dietary Fiber: 2 gm
Sodium: 83 mg

□□□□□□□□□□□□□□□□□□□□

Hawaiian Chicken Salad

Serves: 4

12 oz. chicken breast, cubed
½ cup celery, diced
1 medium apple, chopped
1 cup pineapple chunks, in own juice drained
2 tbsp. plump raisins
3 tbsp. low fat mayonnaise
½ tsp. curry powder

1. Combine chicken, celery, apple, pineapple and raisins in a large bowl.
2. Mix mayonnaise and curry powder.
3. Pour mayonnaise mixture over chicken mixture and toss to coat.

Serving Size: 1 cup
Exchanges per Serving: 3 Meat, 1 Fruit, 1 Fat

Nutrition Facts

Calories: 243
Total Fat: 5 gm
Saturated Fat: 1.5 gm
Polyunsaturated Fat: 2 gm
Monounsaturated Fat: 2 gm

Cholesterol: 78 mg
Protein: 28 gm
Carbohydrate: 19 gm
Dietary Fiber: 2 gm
Sodium: 143 mg

Marinated Beef Skewers

Serves: 6

1 lb. shoulder steak, trimmed
1 tbsp. lemon juice
1 garlic clove, minced
1 tsp. oregano
1 tbsp. olive oil
¼ cup red cooking wine
¼ cup parsley, chopped
18 cherry tomatoes, optional

1. Cut beef crosswise into 18 (1/8 inch) pieces. Place into large food storage bag.
2. Combine lemon juice, garlic, oregano, olive oil, cooking wine, and parsley in a bowl; mix well.
3. Pour marinade over beef in storage bag. Marinate in refrigerator for at least 30 minutes or more.
4. Meanwhile, soak 18 (6 inch) wooden skewers in water for 20 minutes.
5. Preheat grill. Remove beef from marinade. Weave beef strips onto skewers.
6. Grill 4-5 minutes on each side, or until desired doneness.

Serving Size: 3 skewers
Exchanges per Serving: 3 Meats

Nutrition Facts

Calories: 165
Total Fat: 8 gm
Saturated Fat: 2.5 gm
Polyunsaturated Fat: 0.5 gm
Monounsaturated Fat: 4 gm

Cholesterol: 59 mg
Protein: 20 gm
Carbohydrate: 1 gm
Dietary Fiber: 0 gm
Sodium: 47 mg

Matzoh Stuffed Chicken Cutlets

Serves: 10

10 (5 oz.) boneless chicken breasts

Stuffing:
½ tsp. olive oil
½ cup chopped onion
5 whole wheat matzoh boards, finely broken
½ cup medium dry Concord wine
½ cup low sodium chicken broth
1 egg white
½ tbsp. paprika
¼ tsp. pepper

Sauce:
1/3 cup low fat mayonnaise
2 tbsp. ketchup
1 tbsp. honey

1. Sauté onion in olive oil until tender, but not browned.
2. Add broken matzohs and toast lightly.
3. Combine wine, egg white, seasonings, and chicken broth to matzoh mixture.
4. Mix well until matzoh is soft and mixture is heated through.
5. Take ¼ cup of stuffing, place in the middle of each chicken cutlet and roll. Secure with a toothpick, if needed.
6. Combine mayonnaise, ketchup, and honey in a bowl. Mix well. Spread on top of chicken cutlet rolls.
7. Bake at 350 degrees F for 30 to 40 minutes.

Serving Size: 1 (4 oz.) stuffed chicken cutlet
Exchanges per Serving: 4 Meat, 1 Starch, ½ Fat

□□□□□□□□□□□□□□□□□□□□

Nutrition Facts

Calories: 266
Total Fat: 4.5 gm
Saturated Fat: 1 gm
Polyunsaturated Fat: 0.5 gm
Monounsaturated Fat: 0.5 gm

Cholesterol: 83 mg
Protein: 36 gm
Carbohydrate: 17 gm
Dietary Fiber: 2 gm
Sodium: 198 mg

□□□□□□□□□□□□□□□□□□□□

Oven "Fried" Coated Chicken

Serves: 4

1 (2-2 ½ lbs.) chicken
4 tbsp. fat free Italian dressing
1 tsp. garlic powder
1 tsp. onion powder
¾ cup matzoh meal

1. Cut up chicken, remove skin, and as much fat as possible.
2. Dip chicken in fat free Italian dressing and then coat with matzoh meal seasoned with garlic and onion powder.
3. Lightly spray chicken with non-stick cooking spray.
4. Bake chicken at 350 degrees F for 45-60 minutes.

Serving Size: 4 oz. chicken
Exchanges per Serving: 4 Meat, 1 Starch

Nutrition Facts:

Calories: 284
Total Fat: 5 gm
Saturated Fat: 1.5 gm
Polyunsaturated Fat: 1.5 gm
Monounsaturated Fat: 1.5 gm

Cholesterol: 115 mg
Protein: 38 gm
Carbohydrate: 18 gm
Dietary Fiber: 1 gm
Sodium: 127 mg

Savory Sweet Chicken

Serves: 4

1 large onion, chopped
1 ½ tsp. olive oil
1 whole chicken, quartered, no skin
¼ tsp. ginger
½ tsp. cinnamon
¼ cup reduced or sugar-free apricot jam
1 cup orange juice
Juice of one lemon (~2 ½ tbsp.)
2 cups fat free, low sodium chicken broth, or water
10 large prunes, pitted
½ cup dried apricots
Pepper to taste

1. Sauté onion in large pot in olive oil until soft, but not browned.
2. Mix ginger and cinnamon and sprinkle on chicken pieces.
3. Place chicken in the pot with the onions, and brown on all sides.
4. In a separate bowl, mix together all other ingredients except pepper.
5. Pour mixture over chicken.
6. Cook over a low flame for at least 40 minutes. Add more broth if necessary.
7. Add pepper to taste.

Serving Size: ¼ chicken (~ 4 oz.)
Exchanges per Serving: 4 Meat, 2 Fruit

Nutrition Facts

Calories: 350
Total Fat: 7 gm
Saturated Fat: 1.5 gm
Polyunsaturated Fat: 2 gm
Monounsaturated Fat: 2.5 gm

Cholesterol: 115 mg
Protein: 38 gm
Carbohydrate: 36 gm
Dietary Fiber: 3 gm
Sodium: 163 mg

Stuffed Chicken Matzoh Roll

Serves: 20

10 "prepared" matzoh
1 tbsp. olive oil
2 lbs. chicken breast
2 onions
5 garlic cloves
3 tbsp. matzoh meal
4 tsp. chili powder
1 ½ tsp. ground cumin
4 cups fat free chicken broth
2 tbsp. tomato paste

1. Heat olive oil in non-stick skillet sprayed with cooking spray. Add chicken and cook for about 7-10 minutes, or until thoroughly cooked, stirring occasionally. Remove chicken from skillet and set aside.
2. Cook onion and garlic with the chicken juices in the skillet for about 5 minutes.
3. Add matzoh meal, chili powder and cumin and let cook for 3 minutes.
4. Stir in chicken broth and tomato paste and let simmer for 5 minutes; add the cooked chicken and remove from heat.
5. Cut matzoh in half. Place a heaping tablespoon of the chicken mixture on the lower part of each matzoh and roll up.
6. Place in 13 x 9 x 2 baking pan sprayed with non-stick cooking spray. Drizzle remaining sauce over the stuffed chicken.
7. Bake in 400 degrees F oven for 15-20 minutes.

Serving Size: 1 stuffed matzoh roll
Exchanges per Serving: 1 Starch, 1 ½ Meat

□□□□□□□□□□□□□□□□□□□□□

Nutrition Facts

Calories: 128
Total Fat: 1.5 gm
Saturated Fat: 0 gm
Polyunsaturated Fat: 0 gm
Monounsaturated Fat: 1 gm

Cholesterol: 26 mg
Protein: 13 gm
Carbohydrate: 16 gm
Dietary Fiber: 1 gm
Sodium: 159 mg

□□□□□□□□□□□□□□□□□□□□□

Tomato Veal Cutlets

Serves: 6

1 cup matzoh meal
1/8 tsp. pepper
2 lbs. veal cutlets
1 (11 oz.) can tomato and mushroom sauce
Non-stick cooking spray

1. Mix matzoh meal with pepper.
2. Dip cutlets in tomato and mushroom sauce, roll in matzoh meal mixture.
3. Chill in refrigerator at least one half hour.
4. Spray large skillet with non-stick cooking spray and cook cutlets, over low heat, until tender and brown.

Serving Size: 1 (4 oz.) cutlet
Exchanges per Serving: 4 Meat, 1 Starch, 1 Vegetable

Nutrition Facts

Calories: 250
Total Fat: 1.5 gm
Saturated Fat: 0.5 gm
Polyunsaturated Fat: 0 gm
Monounsaturated Fat: 0.5 gm

Cholesterol: 156 mg
Protein: 37 gm
Carbohydrate: 20 gm
Dietary Fiber: 1 gm
Sodium: 298 mg

Turkey and Potato Turnovers

Serves: 24

12 "prepared" matzoh
1 tbsp. oil
2 cups onion, chopped
2 cups canned mushrooms, drained & sliced
Salt and pepper to taste
4 egg whites, beaten
1 lb. ground turkey
2 medium potatoes, mashed
1 tbsp. margarine
½ tsp. garlic powder
½ tsp. onion powder

1. Preheat oven to 400 degrees F. Spray a large cookie sheet with non-stick cooking spray. In a large sized skillet, heat the oil and sauté the onions until limp. Add mushrooms, season with salt and pepper, and sauté for ten minutes. Remove from skillet and set aside.
2. Place ground turkey into skillet, season with salt and pepper and brown by thoroughly cooking the turkey. Add the mushroom mixture to the browned turkey and cook for about five minutes.
3. Remove turkey mixture from the heat and add mashed potatoes mixed with margarine and mix well. Season with garlic powder, onion powder, and if necessary, with salt and pepper to taste.
4. Cut prepared matzoh into fourths.
5. Place about one tablespoon of turkey mixture in the center of each quarter and fold cut side diagonally over to close and form a triangle.
6. Place turnovers onto sprayed cookie sheet. Using a pastry brush, lightly brush tops of turnovers with beaten egg white.
7. Place turnovers into preheated oven and bake for approximately 30 minutes.

Serving Size: 2 turnovers
Exchanges per Serving: 1 Starch, 1 Meat

□□□□□□□□□□□□□□□□□□□□□

Nutrition Facts

Calories: 115
Total Fat: 3 gm
Saturated Fat: 0.5 gm
Polyunsaturated Fat: 0.5 gm
Monounsaturated Fat: 1 gm

Cholesterol: 15 mg
Protein: 6 gm
Carbohydrate: 17 gm
Dietary Fiber: 1 gm
Sodium: 117 mg

□□□□□□□□□□□□□□□□□□□□□

Turkey Goulash

Serves: 14

1 tsp. olive oil
2 garlic cloves, crushed
1 large onion, sliced
2 lbs. boneless turkey breast
1 tsp. black pepper
1 tsp. paprika
¼ lb. mushrooms
2 medium carrots, cut into chunks
2 stalks celery, sliced
3 medium potatoes, peeled and cubed
1 ½ cups water
4 tbsp. ketchup
2 tbsp. potato starch

1. Sauté onion and garlic in oil over medium heat until transparent.
2. Cut turkey breast into small cubes. Add turkey cubes, pepper and paprika to sauté pan and roast gently on all sides.
3. Cover and cook over low heat for 30 minutes.
4. Add the rest of the ingredients.
5. Cover and simmer for about an hour until the turkey is tender.
6. If mixture is too thick, add water. If too thin, add 1-2 tbsp of potato starch mixed with ¼ cup of water.
7. Cook for another 10-12 minutes.

Serving Size: 1 cup
Exchanges per Serving: 2 Very Lean Meat, 1 Starch, ½ Vegetable

Nutrition Facts

Calories: 130
Total Fat: 1 gm
Saturated Fat: 0 gm
Polyunsaturated Fat: 0 gm
Monounsaturated Fat: 0 gm

Cholesterol: 40 mg
Protein: 17 gm
Carbohydrate: 13 gm
Dietary Fiber: 1 gm
Sodium: 94 mg

Fish

FISH

Fish Loaf

Serves: 15

2 lbs. flounder fillet
2 stalks celery
3 carrots, sliced
1 medium onion
2 cups water
5 small potatoes, cubed
2 tbsp. low fat margarine
1 egg, beaten
2 egg whites, beaten
½ cup matzoh meal
Salt & pepper to taste

1. Cook the fish, celery, carrots, onion, and potatoes in 2 cups water, until tender, about 10-20 minutes. Water will get absorbed. Drain and mash to a lumpy texture.
2. Add margarine, beaten egg and egg whites, and matzoh meal. Season with salt and pepper to taste.
3. Put in standard size loaf pan and bake at 350 degrees F for 30 to 45 minutes or until brown on top.

Serving Size: 1 piece
Exchanges per Serving: 2 Meat, 1 Starch

□□□□□□□□□□□□□□□□□□□□

Nutrition Facts

Calories: 117
Total Fat: 2 gm
Saturated Fat: 0 gm
Polyunsaturated Fat: 0.5 gm
Monounsaturated Fat: 0.5 gm

Cholesterol: 43 gm
Protein: 14 gm
Carbohydrate: 11 mg
Dietary Fiber: 1 gm
Sodium: 245 mg

□□□□□□□□□□□□□□□□□□□□

Grilled Cod
with Curried Tomato Sauce

Serves: 4

Non-stick cooking spray
½ tsp. olive oil
1 cup chopped onion
2 tsp. curry powder
2 ½ cups chopped tomato
½ tsp. onion powder
2 tbsp. chopped fresh basil
¼ tsp. sugar
¼ tsp. pepper
4 (6 oz.) cod fillets

1. Coat a large saucepan with non-stick cooking spray. Add the oil; place over medium heat until hot. Add the onion and sauté 5 minutes or until tender. Add the curry powder; cook 1 minute.
2. Stir in tomato, onion powder, basil and sugar; bring to a boil. Reduce heat and simmer, uncovered, 25 minutes or until reduced to 2 cups. Remove from heat.
3. Prepare grill. Sprinkle pepper over fish. Place fish on grill rack coated with cooking spray; grill 5 minutes on each side or until fish flakes easily when tested with a fork. Top with ½ cup curried tomato sauce.

Serving Size: 1 fillet
Exchanges per Serving: 4 ½ Meat, 1 ½ Vegetable

Nutrition Facts

Calories: 185
Total fat: 2 gm
Saturated Fat: 0 gm
Polyunsaturated Fat: 0.5 gm
Monounsaturated Fat: 1 gm

Cholesterol: 73 mg
Protein: 32 gm
Carbohydrate: 9 gm
Dietary Fiber: 2 gm
Sodium: 100 mg

Poached Chilean Sea Bass

Serves: 4

1 ½ cups white wine
½ cup water
2 tbsp. lemon juice
1 bay leaf
½ tsp. salt
½ tsp. dried thyme
½ tsp. dried basil
¼ tsp. black pepper
4 (4 oz.) Chilean Sea Bass fillets
1 small onion, sliced
1 medium tomato, sliced
½ cup mushrooms, sliced

1. Combine first 8 ingredients in a 10 inch skillet, stirring well. Bring mixture to a boil.
2. Reduce heat; cover and simmer 10 minutes.
3. Layer fillets, onion, tomato, and mushrooms in wine mixture. Cover and simmer 8 minutes or until fish flakes easily when tested with a fork.
4. Transfer fish and vegetables to a serving platter.

Serving Size: 1 fillet
Exchanges per Serving: 3 ½ Meat, ½ Vegetable

Nutrition Facts

Calories: 190
Total Fat: 0 gm
Saturated Fat: 0 gm
Polyunsaturated Fat: 0 gm
Monounsaturated Fat: 0 gm

Cholesterol: 0 mg
Protein: 24 gm
Carbohydrate: 7 gm
Dietary Fiber: 1 gm
Sodium: 299 mg

Salmon Cakes
with Yogurt Dill Sauce

Serves: 4

6 small red potatoes (~1 lb.)
2 cups salmon, canned in water
2 egg whites
4 scallions, chopped
2 tbsp. parsley, chopped
2 tsp. olive oil

Yogurt Dill Sauce:
¼ cup non fat plain yogurt
¼ cup light mayonnaise
2 tbsp. dill
¼ tsp. salt

1. Halve potatoes with the skin on and place in a small saucepan with ½ cup of water. Bring to a boil; reduce heat and simmer until potatoes are tender, about 15 minutes. Remove potatoes and mash with a fork.
2. Combine the mashed potatoes with salmon, egg whites, scallions and parsley.
3. Heat the olive oil in a non-stick skillet over medium heat. Measure ½ cup portions of salmon mixture and form into patties. Cook about 4 minutes on each side.
4. Mix together yogurt dill sauce ingredients. Top each salmon cake with 2 tablespoons of sauce.

Serving Size: 1 salmon cake with 2 tablespoons yogurt dill sauce
Exchanges per Serving: 2 Meat, 1 Starch, 1 Fat

□□□□□□□□□□□□□□□□□□□□□□

Nutrition Facts:

Calories: 190
Total Fat: 10 gm
Saturated Fat: 1.5 gm
Polyunsaturated Fat: 4 gm
Monounsaturated Fat: 3.5 gm

Cholesterol: 46 mg
Protein: 17 gm
Carbohydrate: 19 gm
Dietary Fiber: 2 gm
Sodium: 264 mg

□□□□□□□□□□□□□□□□□□□□□□

NOTE: You can decrease total fat content by using 1 tablespoon Yogurt Dill Sauce and count as ½ fat exchange.

Tuna "Noodle" Casserole

Serves: 8

8 "prepared" matzoh
¾ cup mushrooms
¼ cup red peppers
2 tbsp. onions
1 ½ tbsp. margarine
3 tbsp. potato starch
2 cup fat free milk
¼ tsp. salt
1/8 tsp. pepper
12.5 oz. canned tuna
2 oz. low fat shredded cheese
¼ cup Passover bread crumbs

1. Cut the prepared matzoh into ½ inch strips, resembling extra wide egg noodles and set aside.
2. Coat saucepan with cooking spray and sauté mushrooms, red pepper and onion for 3 minutes. Remove from saucepan and set aside.
3. Heat margarine until melted; add potato starch and stir constantly with wire whisk for 1 minute.
4. Gradually add milk, stirring constantly until thickened and bubbly; stir in mushroom mixture, matzoh noodles, tuna, salt and pepper.
5. Spoon into shallow baking dish coated with cooking spray.
6. Top with shredded cheese and Passover bread crumbs.
7. Cover and bake at 350 degrees F for 30 minutes.

Serving Size: 1 cup
Exchanges per Serving: 2 Meat, 2 Starch, 1 Fat

□□□□□□□□□□□□□□□□□□□□

Nutrition Facts

Calories: 259
Total Fat: 6 gm
Saturated Fat: 2 gm
Polyunsaturated Fat: 1.5 gm
Monounsaturated Fat: 1 gm

Cholesterol: 25 mg
Protein: 19 gm
Carbohydrate: 34 gm
Dietary Fiber: 1 gm
Sodium: 427 mg

□□□□□□□□□□□□□□□□□□□□

Tuna Patties

Serves: 4

2 cans (6.5 oz. each) tuna, water packed, drained
½ cup onions, finely chopped
½ cup carrots, shredded
1 cup celery, sliced
¼ tsp. pepper
¼ cup fresh parsley, finely chopped
2 tsp. horseradish
2 egg whites
½ cup matzoh meal

1. In a bowl, combine all of the ingredients.
2. Spray a non-stick skillet with non-stick cooking spray. Form the tuna mixture into patties and brown at medium-high heat on both sides until crisp.

Serving Size: 1 patty
Exchanges per Serving: 3 ½ Meat, 1 Starch

🔲🔲🔲🔲🔲🔲🔲🔲🔲🔲🔲🔲🔲🔲🔲🔲🔲🔲🔲

Nutrition Facts

Calories: 212
Total Fat: 3 gm
Saturated Fat: 1 gm
Polyunsaturated Fat: 1 gm
Monounsaturated Fat: 1 gm

Cholesterol: 39 mg
Protein: 26 gm
Carbohydrates: 19 gm
Dietary Fiber: 2 gm
Sodium: 416 mg

🔲🔲🔲🔲🔲🔲🔲🔲🔲🔲🔲🔲🔲🔲🔲🔲🔲🔲🔲

Vegetables

VEGETABLES

Cabbage and Veggie Rolls

Serves: 24

12 "prepared" matzoh
1 tbsp. olive oil
3 medium onions, grated
4 stalks celery, finely sliced
4 medium carrots, peeled and grated
1 small cabbage, grated
1 tbsp. black pepper
4 tbsp. margarine, softened

1. Preheat oven to 400 degrees F.
2. In medium size, non-stick skillet, place oil over medium heat. Sauté onions, celery, carrots, and cabbage for about five to ten minutes. After all vegetables have become limp, add black pepper and continue to sauté for an additional two minutes. Let cool and set aside.
3. Cut "prepared" matzoh into fourths. Lightly brush softened margarine on outside of "prepared" matzoh quarters. Place about one tablespoon of cabbage mixture in lower center of matzoh end and roll up firmly. Place one roll at a time onto 12x17x2 inch pan sprayed with non-stick cooking spray, seam side down. Bake for about 30-40 minutes, or until golden.

Serving Size: 2 rolls
Exchanges per Serving: 1 Starch, 1 Vegetable, ½ Fat

Nutrition Facts

Calories: 97
Total Fat: 3 gm
Saturated Fat: 0 gm
Polyunsaturated Fat: 1 gm
Monounsaturated Fat: 1 gm

Cholesterol: 0 mg
Protein: 2 gm
Carbohydrate: 17 gm
Dietary Fiber: 2 gm
Sodium: 45 mg

Marinated Carrots

Serves: 4

6 carrots (3/4 lb.) cut into ¼ by 2 inch julienne pieces
4 cloves garlic, peeled and crushed
1 tbsp. balsamic vinegar
2 tsp. olive oil
2 tsp. chopped fresh thyme or ½ tsp. dried thyme leaves
Pinch of sugar
Black pepper to taste

1. Place carrots, garlic, and ¼ cup water in a 1 quart casserole dish; cover and microwave on high power for 5 to 7 minutes, stirring midway, or until crisp-tender.
2. Immediately drain the carrots and garlic; transfer to a medium-sized bowl.
3. Add vinegar, oil, thyme, and sugar and toss well.
4. Let cool for 10 minutes, stirring occasionally.
5. Discard the garlic cloves and season with pepper.

Serving Size: ½ cup
Exchanges per Serving: 2 Vegetable, ½ Fat

Nutrition Facts

Calories: 69
Total Fat: 2.5 gm
Saturated Fat: 0 gm
Polyunsaturated Fat: 0 gm
Monounsaturated Fat: 1.5 gm

Cholesterol: 0 mg
Protein: 1 gm
Carbohydrate: 11 gm
Dietary Fiber: 3 gm
Sodium: 65 mg

Stuffed Mushrooms

Serves: 6

1 lb. mushrooms
1 tbsp. olive oil
1 (10 oz.) package frozen chopped spinach
2 egg whites
½ cup matzoh meal
2 cloves of garlic
1 tsp. black pepper

1. Wash mushrooms and remove caps. Sauté whole caps quickly in oil. Chop mushroom stems.
2. Cook spinach according to package directions along with chopped mushroom stems. Drain and squeeze spinach to eliminate excess water; combine with egg whites, matzoh meal, garlic and pepper.
3. Fill mushrooms caps with the spinach mixture. Place caps in a baking dish sprayed with non-stick cooking spray.
4. Bake at 350 degrees F for 10-15 minutes.

Serving Size: 4 stuffed mushrooms
Exchanges per Serving: 1 ½ Vegetable, ½ Starch, ½ Fat

Nutrition Facts

Calories: 101
Total Fat: 3 gm
Saturated Fat: 0 gm
Polyunsaturated Fat: 0 gm
Monounsaturated Fat: 1.5 gm

Cholesterol: 0 mg
Protein: 6 gm
Carbohydrate: 14 gm
Dietary Fiber: 3 gm
Sodium: 57 mg

Sweet and Sour Cabbage

Serves: 12

1 medium head cabbage (red or green), core removed and shredded
1 medium onion, chopped
1 tbsp. olive oil
¼ cup raisins
¼ cup craisins
1 green apple, cored and grated
1 cup water
1 tbsp. matzoh meal
2 tbsp. vinegar
1 tbsp. sugar

1. Heat olive oil in a large pot. Sauté shredded cabbage and onion.
2. Add remaining ingredients and mix well.
3. Cover and cook on low to medium high heat for 20 to 30 minutes.

Serving Size: 1 cup
Exchanges per Serving: 1 Vegetable, ½ Fruit

Nutrition Facts

Calories: 64
Total Fat: 1.5 gm
Saturated Fat: 0 gm
Polyunsaturated Fat: 0 gm
Monounsaturated Fat: 1 gm

Cholesterol: 0 mg
Protein: 1 gm
Carbohydrate: 13 gm
Dietary Fiber: 3 gm
Sodium: 15 mg

Tzimmes

Serves: 15

24 medium carrots, peeled, and sliced diagonally into 1 inch pieces
2 lbs. sweet potatoes, peeled and sliced into 2 inch circles
9 large pitted prunes, cut into thirds
½ cup honey
1 tbsp. ground cinnamon
Freshly grated nutmeg to taste
1 ½ cup water

1. Preheat the oven to 350 degrees F. Coat a 10 x 15 inch Pyrex dish with non-stick cooking spray.
2. Layer the carrots, sweet potatoes, and prunes alternately in the prepared pan, drizzling with honey and sprinkling with the spices. Add water to cover the ingredients. Cover and bake 30 minutes.
3. Uncover and bake 30 additional minutes, or until the carrots and sweet potatoes are soft and the liquid is reduced to a thick and slightly sticky consistency.

Serving Size: 1 cup
Exchanges per Serving: 1 Starch, 1 ½ Vegetables, ½ Fruit

Nutrition Facts

Calories: 140
Total fat: 0 gm
Saturated fat: 0 gm
Polyunsaturated fat: 0 gm
Monounsaturated fat: 0 gm

Cholesterol: 0 mg
Protein: 2 gm
Carbohydrate: 34 gm
Dietary fiber: 5 gm
Sodium: 101 mg

Vegetable Medley Bake

Serves: 9

1 onion, chopped
2 cups (~8 oz.) mushrooms, sliced
1 cup zucchini, diced
2 (10-ounce) boxes frozen, chopped spinach
½ cup matzoh meal
1 large egg
4 egg whites, lightly beaten
¾ cup egg substitute
2 cups carrots, grated or diced
¼ tsp. salt
¼ tsp. black pepper
2 tsp. low-sodium chicken broth powder

1. Preheat oven to 325 degrees F.
2. Coat a large non-stick pan with non-stick cooking spray. Add mushrooms and onions, cover pan, and let cook over medium heat. Stir occasionally until mushrooms are lightly browned.
3. In a large bowl, mix together all remaining ingredients. Add mushroom mixture and mix thoroughly.
4. Spread into a 9x9 inch pan sprayed with cooking spray and bake until firm and lightly browned, approximately 45-60 minutes.

Serving Size: 1 piece
Exchanges per Serving: ½ Meat, 1 ½ Vegetable, ½ Starch

Nutrition Facts

Calories: 103
Total Fat: 1.5 gm
Saturated Fat: 0 gm
Polyunsaturated Fat: 0.5 gm
Monounsaturated Fat: 0 gm

Cholesterol: 24 gm
Protein: 8 gm
Carbohydrate: 14 mg
Dietary Fiber: 3 gm
Sodium: 241 mg

Vegetable Patties

Serves: 8

2 cups minced red or yellow pepper, or a mixture of both
1 tsp. olive oil
1 ½ cup grated carrots (~4 carrots)
½ lb. raw spinach, cleaned, trimmed of coarse stems, and chopped
(2 tightly packed cups)
1 lb. (3 medium) potatoes, boiled and mashed (2 cups)
6 tbsp. (1 large) grated raw onion
1 whole egg
6 egg whites
1 tsp. salt
Freshly ground black pepper
1 cup matzoh meal

1. Sauté peppers in olive oil until soft, about 15-20 minutes.
2. Add all of the remaining ingredients; place in refrigerator for 30
    minutes. Bring to room temperature before continuing.
3. Form each patty with approximately ¼ cup of the mixture.
4. Place the patties on a baking sheet sprayed with non-stick
    cooking spray, flattening them slightly.
5. Bake in a preheated 350 degree F oven for about 10 minutes;
    turn the patties and bake for another 7-10 minutes.

Serving Size: 5 patties
Exchanges per Serving: 2 Starch, 1 Vegetable

Nutrition Facts

Calories: 171
Total Fat: 2 gm
Saturated Fat: 0 gm
Polyunsaturated Fat: 0 gm
Monounsaturated Fat: 0.5 gm

Cholesterol: 26 mg
Protein: 7 gm
Carbohydrate: 32 gm
Dietary Fiber: 4 gm
Sodium: 383 mg

Zucchini and Mushroom Sauté

Serves: 6

1 medium onion, chopped
2 garlic cloves
1 medium tomato, diced
2 small zucchini, trimmed and cut into ¼ inch julienne pieces
1 ½ cup sliced mushrooms (4 oz.)
2 tsp. chopped fresh basil or ½ tsp. dried
Black pepper to taste

1. In a large non-stick skillet sprayed with non-stick cooking spray, sauté onion, garlic, and tomato for 2 minutes.
2. Add zucchini and sauté for 5 minutes.
3. Add mushrooms and basil and sauté just until the vegetables have softened.
4. Season with pepper and herbs of your choice.

Serving Size: ½ cup
Exchanges per Serving: 1 ½ Vegetable

Nutrition Facts

Calories: 36
Total Fat: 0 gm
Saturated Fat: 0 gm
Polyunsaturated Fat: 0 gm
Monounsaturated Fat: 0 gm

Cholesterol: 0 mg
Protein: 3 gm
Carbohydrate: 7 gm
Dietary Fiber: 2 gm
Sodium: 14 mg

Side Dishes

SIDE DISHES

Acorn Squash with Apple Filling

Serves: 4

2 acorn squash (~1 ¼ lb.)
Cinnamon

Stuffing:
¼ cup raisins
¼ cup sweet wine
3 medium apples
1 tbsp. light margarine
¼ cup brown sugar
1 tbsp. lemon juice

1. Halve the squashes and scoop out the seeds and stringy interiors.
2. Trim undersides so halves will sit flat. Sprinkle cut surfaces with cinnamon.
3. Place in baking pan with cut sides down. Put ½ cup water in pan, or enough to just cover the bottom of the pan.
4. Bake squash 30 minutes in preheated 350 degree F oven.
5. While squash is baking, soak raisins in wine to plump.
6. Chop apples to ½ inch cubes, peeled or unpeeled.
7. In small sauté pan, melt margarine and add apples. Cook 3-5 minutes, until slightly wilted.
8. Stir in sugar and lemon juice.
9. When squash has cooked 30 minutes, turn cut sides up. Drain raisins, add to apple mixture.
10. Fill squash cavities with apple mixture. Cover and bake 20-30 minutes more or until tender.

Serving Size: ½ squash
Exchanges per Serving: 1 ½ Starch, 1 ½ Fruit

□□□□□□□□□□□□□□□□□□□□□□□

Nutrition Facts

Calories: 208
Total Fat: 1.5 gm
Saturated Fat: 0 gm
Polyunsaturated Fat: 0 gm
Monounsaturated Fat: 0.5 gm

Cholesterol: 0 mg
Protein: 2 gm
Carbohydrate: 47 gm
Dietary Fiber: 5 gm
Sodium: 30 mg

□□□□□□□□□□□□□□□□□□□□□□□

Apple Stuffing

Serves: 16

1 large onion
1 medium green bell pepper
2 garlic cloves
¾ cup matzoh meal
¼ tsp. black pepper
1/8 tsp. cinnamon
2 stalks celery, diced
2 eggs
4 egg whites
1 apple, peeled and diced
½ cup raisins
1 tbsp. honey

1. Sauté onion, green pepper and garlic in a non-stick pan for 5 minutes.
2. Remove from heat and stir in remaining ingredients.
3. Pour into 8 X 8 square pan sprayed with non-stick cooking spray. Bake in 350 degree F oven for 30 minutes or until browned.

Serving Size: 1 piece
Exchanges per Serving: ½ Starch, ½ Fruit

□□□□□□□□□□□□□□□□□□□□

Nutrition Facts

Calories: 66
Total Fat: 0.5 gm
Saturated Fat: 0 gm
Polyunsaturated Fat: 0 gm
Monounsaturated Fat: 0 gm

Cholesterol: 26 mg
Protein: 3 gm
Carbohydrate: 13 gm
Dietary Fiber: 1 gm
Sodium: 28 mg

□□□□□□□□□□□□□□□□□□□□

Carrot and Parsnip Latkes

Serves: 8

2 medium carrots, peeled and coarsely shredded
5 small parsnips (~ 1 lb.), peeled and coarsely shredded
¼ cup matzoh meal
4 egg whites, beaten
1 tsp. chopped scallions
1 tsp. chopped parsley
1/8 tsp. salt
1/8 tsp. black pepper
1 tsp. oil

1. In large bowl, toss carrots and parsnips with matzoh meal. Add egg whites, scallions, parsley, salt and pepper. Mix until evenly moistened.
2. In 12-inch skillet, heat 1 tsp. oil and non-stick cooking spray over medium-high heat. With hands, press together about ¼ cup of vegetable mixture; place in skillet and flatten with a wide metal spatula. Repeat with rest of vegetable mixture.
3. Cook latkes about 5 minutes, turning once, until browned on both sides.

Serving Size: 2 latkes
Exchanges per Serving: 1 Starch

Nutrition Facts

Calories: 76
Total Fat: 1 gm
Saturated Fat: 0 gm
Polyunsaturated Fat: 0 gm
Monounsaturated Fat: 0 gm

Cholesterol: 0 mg
Protein: 3 gm
Carbohydrate: 15 gm
Dietary Fiber: 2 gm
Sodium: 44 mg

Charoset

Serves: 5

2 apples, cored and chopped
¼ cup walnuts, chopped
½ tsp. cinnamon
1 tsp. ground ginger
2 tbsp. sweet red wine

1. Combine all ingredients in a food processor and gently blend.
2. Allow to chill for at least 1 hour before serving.

Serving Size: ¼ cup
Exchanges per Serving: ½ Fruit, 1 Fat

Nutrition Facts

Calories: 74
Total Fat: 4 gm
Saturated Fat: 0 gm
Polyunsaturated Fat: 2 gm
Monounsaturated Fat: 1 gm

Cholesterol: 0 mg
Protein: 2 gm
Carbohydrate: 9 gm
Dietary Fiber: 2 gm
Sodium: 1 mg

Farfel Kishka

Serves: 10

2 tbsp. olive oil
1 large sweet onion, diced
2 carrots, grated
2 celery stalks, diced
2 garlic cloves, minced
3 cups matzoh farfel
½ cup matzoh meal
1 tsp. salt
¼ tsp. pepper
¼ tsp. poultry seasoning
4 egg whites
Garnish: parsley sprig

1. Heat olive oil in a large skillet over medium-high heat; add onion, carrot, celery, and garlic, and sauté 5 to 6 minutes or until tender. Stir in matzoh farfel and next 4 ingredients; let cool.
2. Add beaten egg whites, stirring mixture until well blended.
3. Shape mixture into a 12 inch roll and place on a piece of heavy duty aluminum foil. Fold sides of foil loosely over roll; fold ends over, and crimp to seal. Place on a baking pan.
4. Bake at 350 degrees F for 45 minutes. Unwrap and cut into ½ inch thick slices.

Serving Size: 1 slice
Exchanges per Serving: 1 ½ Starch, ½ Vegetable, ½ Fat

Nutrition Facts

Calories: 154
Total Fat: 3 gm
Saturated Fat: 0 gm
Polyunsaturated Fat: 0 gm
Monounsaturated Fat: 2 gm

Cholesterol: 0 mg
Protein: 5 gm
Carbohydrate: 26 gm
Dietary Fiber: 1 gm
Sodium: 272 mg

Farfel Ring

Serves: 12

4 cups fat free, low sodium chicken broth
14 oz. matzoh farfel
1 tbsp. olive oil
1 large onion, peeled and minced
½ lb. fresh mushrooms, cleaned and sliced
½ cup Italian flat-leaf parsley
½ tsp. ground white pepper
Pinch of salt (~1/8 tsp. salt)

1. Bring the chicken broth to a boil in a saucepan; add the farfel and simmer over medium heat until almost dry.
2. Heat the olive oil in a non-stick sauté pan over medium heat. Add the onion and sauté for 5 minutes, or until wilted. Add the mushrooms and sauté 2 to 3 minutes.
3. Add the farfel to the mushroom-onion mixture. Blend. Add the parsley and pepper. Add a pinch of salt. Heat the oven to 350 degrees F.
4. Coat a 2 ½ quart ring mold with non-stick cooking spray. Add the farfel mixture and cover with foil.
5. Place the mold in a large baking pan. Fill the pan with 1 inch of hot water, place in the oven, and bake for 1 hour.
6. Remove the mold from the water bath and let stand for 15 minutes. Loosen the edges of the farfel ring with a spatula, and unmold.

To Serve: Unmold the ring on a round platter and fill the center with desired vegetables.

Serving Size: 1 slice
Exchanges per Serving: 2 Starch

□□□□□□□□□□□□□□□□□□□□□□

Nutrition Facts

Calories: 141

Total Fat: 1 gm

Saturated Fat: 0 gm

Polyunsaturated Fat: 0 gm

Monounsaturated Fat: 1 gm

Cholesterol: 0 mg

Protein: 5 gm

Carbohydrate: 29 gm

Dietary Fiber: 2 gm

Sodium: 47 mg

□□□□□□□□□□□□□□□□□□□□□□

Matzoh Brei

Serves: 3

3 matzoh boards
1 tbsp. olive oil
2 eggs
¼ tsp. black pepper
2 tbsp. water

1. Break matzoh into pieces.
2. Cover with water, draining immediately. Press excess water out of matzoh.
3. Heat the oil in a non-stick skillet.
4. Add matzoh and sauté until lightly browned.
5. Beat eggs with 2 tbsp. water and pepper.
6. Pour over matzoh in pan and stir frequently, until eggs are set.

Serving Size: 1 cup
Exchanges per Serving: 1 ½ Starch, ½ Meat, 1 Fat

Nutrition Facts

Calories: 200
Total Fat: 8 gm
Saturated Fat: 1.5 gm
Polyunsaturated Fat: 2 gm
Monounsaturated Fat: 4 gm

Cholesterol: 140 mg
Protein: 7 gm
Carbohydrate: 24 gm
Dietary Fiber: 1 gm
Sodium: 45 mg

Matzoh Farfel Casserole

Serves: 8

2 tsp. olive oil
1 medium onion, minced
1 tsp. kosher salt
1 (4 oz) can sliced mushrooms, drained
3 ½ cups matzoh farfel
1 cup low sodium chicken broth
1 large egg
2 egg whites
1 cup celery, diced
¼ tsp. ground pepper
1 tsp. paprika
2 cups hot water

1. Preheat oven to 375 degrees F. Heat oil in a large skillet over medium-high heat. Sauté onion and celery until tender (~11 minutes). Let cool slightly.
2. Stir in mushrooms and matzoh farfel.
3. Mix chicken broth, egg, egg whites, salt, pepper, and paprika in a medium bowl. Add to matzoh mixture and blend thoroughly. Stir in 2 cups of hot water.
4. Pour into a 11x7 inch baking dish sprayed with non-stick cooking spray and bake for 40 minutes, or until browned and set.

Serving Size: 1 piece
Exchanges per Serving: 2 Starch

Nutrition Facts

Calories: 161
Total Fat: 2 gm
Saturated Fat: 0 gm
Polyunsaturated Fat: 0 gm
Monounsaturated Fat: 1 gm

Cholesterol: 26 mg
Protein: 6 gm
Carbohydrate: 28 gm
Dietary Fiber: 1 gm
Sodium: 334 mg

Mock Kishka

Serves: 12 (6 slices per roll)

4 carrots
1 onion
2 celery stalks
8 oz. matzoh crackers (2 cups processed)
Pepper to taste
2 tbsp. oil

1. Combine all ingredients except oil in food processor. Process, then add oil.
2. Continue to process and form into 2 rolls. Wrap each roll in foil.
3. Bake for 40 minutes at 375 degrees F.

Serving Size: 1 slice
Exchanges per Serving: 1 Starch, ½ Vegetable, ½ Fat

Nutrition Facts

Calories: 109
Total Fat: 2.5 gm
Saturated Fat: 0 gm
Polyunsaturated Fat: 2 gm
Monounsaturated Fat: 0 gm

Cholesterol: 0 mg
Protein: 2 gm
Carbohydrate: 19 gm
Dietary Fiber: 1 gm
Sodium: 20 mg

"Noodles"

Serves: 12

1 cup egg substitute
1 egg white
1/3 cup hot water
¼ cup potato starch
Pinch of salt

1. Beat egg substitute and egg white with salt and set aside.
2. Dissolve potato starch in hot water; mix well with beaten egg mixture.
3. Coat an 8 inch skillet with non-stick cooking spray.
4. Drop slightly less than ¼ cup into pan, spreading quickly to cover bottom of the pan. When golden, turn over.
5. Roll up and cut into strips. Repeat with rest of batter.

Serving Size: ¼ cup "noodles"
Exchanges per Serving: ½ Meat, ¼ Starch

□□□□□□□□□□□□□□□□□□□□□□□

Nutrition Facts

Calories: 48
Total Fat: 1 gm
Saturated Fat: 0 gm
Polyunsaturated Fat: 0.5 gm
Monounsaturated Fat: 0 gm

Cholesterol: 0 mg
Protein: 4 gm
Carbohydrate: 5 gm
Dietary Fiber: 0 gm
Sodium: 99 mg

□□□□□□□□□□□□□□□□□□□□□□□

Parsnips with Sautéed Onions

Serves: 8

2 tsp. olive oil
4 onions, thinly sliced (~4 cups)
1 tbsp. dried thyme
½ tsp. salt
1/8 tsp. black pepper
1 ½ lbs. parsnips, peeled and thinly sliced (~8 parsnips)
1 cup reduced sodium chicken or vegetable broth

1. Preheat oven to 400 degrees F. Coat a 1 ½ quart shallow baking dish with non-stick cooking spray.
2. Heat oil in a large non-stick skillet over medium-high heat. Add onions and cook, stirring frequently, until golden, 8-10 minutes. Add thyme, salt and pepper; remove from heat.
3. Spread half the parsnips in the prepared dish. Cover with onions. Top with the remaining parsnips and pour in broth. Tightly cover the dish with aluminum foil and bake until the parsnips are very tender, about 1 hour.
4. Remove from the oven. Set the oven to broil. Uncover the dish and baste the top with juices. Broil until the top begins to brown, 3-4 minutes.

Serving Size: 1 cup
Exchanges per Serving: 1 Starch, 1 ½ Vegetable

Nutrition Facts

Calories: 107
Total Fat: 1.5 gm
Saturated Fat: 0 gm
Polyunsaturated Fat: 0 gm
Monounsaturated Fat: 1 gm

Cholesterol: 0 mg
Protein: 2 gm
Carbohydrate: 23 gm
Dietary Fiber: 5 gm
Sodium: 209 mg

Potato Broccoli Knishes

Serves: 6

1 cup mashed potatoes
1/3 cup matzoh meal
2 tbsp. potato starch
½ small onion, finely chopped
2 egg whites
½ tsp. black pepper
¼ tsp. salt
1 cup fresh or frozen broccoli, steamed and finely chopped
Non-stick cooking spray

1. Preheat oven to 375 degrees F.
2. In a bowl, combine the potatoes, matzoh meal, potato starch, onion, egg whites, pepper and salt; knead together.
3. Divide the dough into 6 balls and flatten each.
4. Divide the broccoli evenly onto each circle, fold over, and press edges to seal.
5. Spray a baking sheet with cooking spray. Arrange the knishes in a single layer and place the baking sheet on the bottom rack of the oven.
6. Bake for 15 minutes on each side. Serve hot.

Serving Size: 1 knish
Exchanges per Serving: 1 Starch

Nutrition Facts

Calories: 76
Total Fat: 0 gm
Saturated Fat: 0 gm
Polyunsaturated Fat: 0 gm
Monounsaturated Fat: 0 gm

Cholesterol: 0 mg
Protein: 3 gm
Carbohydrate: 16 gm
Dietary Fiber: 1 gm
Sodium: 122 mg

Potato Croquettes

Serves: 10

1 ½ lbs. potatoes, peeled and chopped
5 cups water
1 onion, peeled and chopped
¼ lb. mushrooms
2 tsp. olive oil
1 tbsp. water
Pepper to taste
Garlic and onion powder to taste
1 cup matzoh meal

1. Boil potatoes in the water until tender. Drain and mash potatoes.
2. In a separate pan, sauté onion and mushrooms in 1 tsp. olive oil and water over medium-high heat for 3 minutes.
3. Mix the mashed potatoes, sautéed onion and mushrooms, seasonings, and matzoh meal together in a large bowl. Form 10 burgers.
4. Brown burgers in non-stick pan sprayed with cooking spray and 1 tsp. olive oil. Cook for 8 minutes; flip over and continue cooking for another 8 minutes.

Serving Size: 1 croquette
Exchanges per Serving: 1 ½ Starch

Nutrition Facts

Calories: 112
Total Fat: 1 gm
Saturated Fat: 0 gm
Polyunsaturated Fat: 0 gm
Monounsaturated Fat: 0.5 gm

Cholesterol: 0 mg
Protein: 3 gm
Carbohydrate: 23 gm
Dietary Fiber: 2 gm
Sodium: 9 mg

Potato Salad

Serves: 12

4 cups cold boiled potatoes, cubed
1 onion, chopped
1 tsp. salt
½ tsp. paprika
2 tbsp. fat-free French dressing
2 tbsp. fat-free mayonnaise
2 hard boiled eggs
2 hard boiled egg whites
2 tsp. parsley, chopped

1. Mix cubed potatoes with chopped onion, salt & paprika.
2. Mix in French dressing and mayonnaise and then chill.
3. Before serving, add eggs, egg whites and parsley. Pile on a bed of leafy greens.

Serving Size: ½ cup
Exchanges per Serving: 1 Starch

□□□□□□□□□□□□□□□□□□□□□

Nutrition Facts

Calories: 85
Total Fat: 1 gm
Saturated Fat: 0 gm
Polyunsaturated Fat: 0 gm
Monounsaturated Fat: 0 gm

Cholesterol: 42 mg
Protein: 3 gm
Carbohydrate: 16 gm
Dietary Fiber: 1 gm
Sodium: 312 mg

□□□□□□□□□□□□□□□□□□□□□

Quinoa with Peppers

Serves: 8

2 tsp. oil
2 onions, chopped
1 green bell pepper, seeded and chopped
1 red bell pepper, seeded and chopped
1 yellow bell pepper, seeded and chopped
2 cloves garlic, crushed
¾ cup uncooked quinoa
4 cups low-sodium vegetable broth
1 tbsp. tomato puree
3 tomatoes, peeled, seeded, and chopped
Italian seasoning to taste

1. Heat the oil in a large skillet over medium-high heat. Add the onions and peppers; cook and stir for about 5 minutes. Add the garlic, and cook for about 2 more minutes. Stir in the quinoa, vegetable broth, and tomato puree.
2. Return to a boil, then cover and simmer over low heat for 20 minutes, or until quinoa grains are soft. Stir in the diced tomatoes and season with Italian seasoning. Cook until heated through, then serve.

Serving Size: ½ cup
Exchanges per Serving: 1 Starch, 1 ½ Vegetable

Nutrition Facts

Calories: 114
Total Fat: 2.5 gm
Saturated Fat: 0 gm
Polyunsaturated Fat: 1.5 gm
Monounsaturated Fat: 0 gm

Cholesterol: 0 mg
Protein: 4 gm
Carbohydrate: 20 gm
Dietary Fiber: 3 gm
Sodium: 76 mg

Vegetable Stuffing

Serves: 18

1 large onion, chopped
1 medium green pepper, chopped
2 garlic cloves, minced
¾ cup matzoh meal
2 carrots, grated
½ cup mushrooms, sliced
¼ tsp. pepper
2 stalks celery, diced
2 eggs
4 egg whites
1 small zucchini, sliced

1. Sauté onion, green pepper, and garlic in non-stick pan for 5 minutes.
2. Remove from heat and stir in the rest of the ingredients.
3. Pour into an 11x7 inch Pyrex dish sprayed with non-stick cooking spray and bake for 30-40 minutes.

Serving Size: 1 piece
Exchanges per Serving: ½ Starch, ½ Vegetable

Nutrition Facts

Calories: 42
Total Fat: 0.5 gm
Saturated Fat: 0 gm
Polyunsaturated Fat: 0 gm
Monounsaturated Fat: 0 gm

Cholesterol: 24 mg
Protein: 3 gm
Carbohydrate: 7 gm
Dietary Fiber: 1 gm
Sodium: 30 mg

Vegetarian Kishka

Serves: 32

4 stalks celery, chopped
2 carrots, grated
2 onions, peeled and minced
2 cups water
2 tbsp. oil
4 cups matzoh meal
1 tbsp. paprika
2 tsp. garlic powder
2 tsp. onion powder
¼ tsp. pepper
1 tsp. salt

1. Process all ingredients together in a food processor.
2. Spoon ¼ of mixture onto a large piece of aluminum foil. Roll mixture in foil into a 6-8 inch roll. Repeat with the remaining mixture to form four rolls.
3. Place aluminum foil rolls on baking sheet and bake in a 350 degree F oven for 45 minutes. Turn rolls over and bake for an additional 45 minutes.
4. Slice and serve.

Serving Size: 1 slice
Exchanges per Serving: 1 Starch, ½ Vegetable

Nutrition Facts

Calories: 81
Total Fat: 1 gm
Saturated Fat: 0 gm
Polyunsaturated Fat: 0 gm
Monounsaturated Fat: 0 gm

Cholesterol: 0 mg
Protein: 2 gm
Carbohydrate: 16 gm
Dietary Fiber: <1 gm
Sodium: 80 mg

Kugels

KUGELS

Apple Kugel

Serves: 8

4 large apples, peeled and grated (~5-6 cups)
2 eggs
4 egg whites
1 cup matzoh meal
2/3 cup yellow raisins
½ cup sugar
2 tbsp. potato starch
1 ½ tsp. cinnamon
1/8 tsp. salt

1. Preheat oven to 350 degrees F.
2. Combine apples, eggs, egg whites, matzoh meal, raisins, sugar, potato starch, cinnamon, and salt in a large bowl. Mix thoroughly.
3. Spoon into an 8 inch baking dish sprayed with non-stick cooking spray, and bake in the oven for 50-55 minutes or until golden.

Serving Size: 1 piece
Exchanges per Serving: 2 Starch, 1 ½ Fruit

Nutrition Facts

Calories: 243
Total Fat: 1.5 gm
Saturated Fat: 0 gm
Polyunsaturated Fat: 0 gm
Monounsaturated Fat: 0 gm

Cholesterol: 53 mg
Protein: 6 gm
Carbohydrate: 54 gm
Dietary Fiber: 4 gm
Sodium: 84 mg

Cabbage Kugel

Serves: 20

3 lbs. cabbage, shredded
2 eggs, separated
6 egg whites
2 tbsp. sugar
1 tbsp. lemon juice
½ cup matzoh meal
Black pepper to taste
Onion and garlic powder to taste

1. Boil cabbage for 25 minutes and drain.
2. Add egg yolks, sugar, and lemon juice.
3. Mix matzoh meal with beaten egg whites and fold into cabbage mixture.
4. Bake at 350 degrees F in a 9x13 inch pan sprayed with non-stick cooking spray.
5. Season with pepper, onion and garlic powders.

Serving Size: 1 piece
Exchanges per Serving: 1 Vegetable, ¼ Starch

Nutrition Facts

Calories: 45
Total Fat: 0.5 gm
Saturated Fat: 0 gm
Polyunsaturated Fat: 0 gm
Monounsaturated Fat: 0 gm

Cholesterol: 21 mg
Protein: 3 gm
Carbohydrate: 8 gm
Dietary Fiber: 2 gm
Sodium: 36 mg

Carrot and Apple Kugel

Serves: 8

8 medium carrots, peeled and grated
3 medium apples, cored, peeled and grated
1 tsp. sugar
½ cup matzo meal
1 tbsp. oil
½ tsp. lemon juice
½ tsp. lemon peel
½ tsp. nutmeg

1. Preheat the oven to 350 degrees F. Spray a round Pyrex dish with non-stick cooking spray.
2. Combine all the ingredients in a bowl and mix well.
3. Transfer the mixture to the prepared baking dish and bake for 20-30 minutes, until browned on top. Serve warm.

Serving Size: 1 piece
Exchanges per Serving: 1 Vegetable, 1 Fruit

Nutrition Facts

Calories: 87
Total Fat: 2 gm
Saturated Fat: 0 gm
Polyunsaturated Fat: 0.5 gm
Monounsaturated Fat: 1 gm

Cholesterol: 0 mg
Protein: 1 gm
Carbohydrate: 17 gm
Dietary Fiber: 3 gm
Sodium: 43 mg

Cauliflower Kugel

Serves: 12

20 oz. frozen cauliflower
1 cup chopped raw onions
1 tsp. olive oil
4 egg whites
2 tbsp. low fat mayonnaise
½ cup matzoh meal
1 tsp. black pepper

1. Steam cauliflower until soft, mash well and set aside.
2. Sauté onions in non-stick spray and 1 tsp. oil.
3. Add onions to cauliflower and mix in the rest of the ingredients.
4. Pour into 9x9 inch square pan sprayed with non-stick cooking spray and bake at 350 degrees F for 30 minutes.

Serving Size: 1 piece
Exchanges per Serving: 2 Vegetables

■□■□■□■□■□■□■□■□■□■□■□■□■

Nutrition Facts

Calories: 52
Total Fat: 1.5 gm
Saturated Fat: 0 gm
Polyunsaturated Fat: 0 gm
Monounsaturated Fat: 0 gm

Cholesterol: 0 mg
Protein: 3 gm
Carbohydrate: 8 gm
Dietary Fiber: 2 gm
Sodium: 50 mg

■□■□■□■□■□■□■□■□■□■□■□■□■

Cinnamon Apple Surprise

Serves: 12

6 medium apples
3 eggs
6 egg whites
¼ tsp. salt
1 ½ cup matzoh meal
1 ½ cups cold water
3 tbsp. oil
¼ cup sugar
1 ½ tsp. cinnamon

1. Peel, core, and slice the apples.
2. Separate the eggs. Beat the egg yolks with the salt, matzoh meal, water, and oil.
3. Beat the egg whites until stiff. Fold into the yolk mixture.
4. Spray a 9x13 inch pan with non-stick cooking spray. Spread half of the batter then layer the apples, sugar, and cinnamon. Top with the other half of the batter.
5. Bake at 350 degrees F for 1 hour.

Serving Size: 1 piece
Exchanges per Serving: 1 Starch, 1 Fruit, 1 Fat

Nutrition Facts

Calories: 159
Total Fat: 5 gm
Saturated Fat: 0.5 gm
Polyunsaturated Fat: 2.5 gm
Monounsaturated Fat: 1 gm

Cholesterol: 53 mg
Protein: 5 gm
Carbohydrate: 24 gm
Dietary Fiber: 1 gm
Sodium: 94 mg

Crisp Potato Kugel

Serves: 12

10 medium potatoes
1 large onion
4 egg whites
1 ½ tsp. salt
Black pepper to taste
2 tbsp. olive oil

1. Grate potatoes and onions and mix together. Add egg whites and salt. Sprinkle black pepper on top of mixture, and set aside.
2. Pour 2 tbsp. olive oil into 8x11 inch Pyrex dish. Place in oven at 400-450 degrees F, until hot.
3. Pour oil into potato mixture. Using a paper towel, wipe out rest of oil from Pyrex dish making sure to coat the bottom and sides of dish.
4. Pour potato mixture into Pyrex dish and bake at 450 degrees F for 45 minutes to 1 hour on top shelf of the oven.

Serving Size: 1 piece
Exchanges per Serving: 1 Starch, ½ Fat

Nutrition Facts

Calories: 102
Total Fat: 2.5 gm
Saturated Fat: 0 gm
Polyunsaturated Fat: 0 gm
Monounsaturated Fat: 1.5 gm

Cholesterol: 0 mg
Protein: 3 gm
Carbohydrate: 18 gm
Dietary Fiber: 2 gm
Sodium: 315 mg

Matzoh Pineapple Kugel

Serves: 16

8 "prepared" matzoh
½ cup orange juice
3 tsp. vanilla extract
3 (16 oz) cans crushed pineapple in own juice, drained
2 eggs
6 egg whites
½ cup sugar
½ tsp. cinnamon

1. Combine orange juice and 1 tsp. vanilla extract in small spray bottle.
2. Take prepared matzoh and spray both sides with orange juice/vanilla mixture.
3. In medium sized bowl, beat egg and egg whites until light and fluffy.
4. Add the sugar, remaining 2 tsp. vanilla extract and cinnamon and mix well. Stir in the drained pineapple and set aside.
5. Arrange two prepared matzohs side by side into 13x9x2 inch baking dish.
6. Spoon 2/3 of pineapple mixture over matzoh and add another layer of matzoh. Repeat this layering, ending with pineapple mixture.
7. Place in 350 degree F preheated oven for about one hour or until the top of the kugel has risen and is golden.

Serving Size: 1 piece
Exchanges per Serving: 1 Starch, 1½ Fruit

Nutrition Facts

Calories: 152
Total Fat: 1 gm
Saturated Fat: 0 gm
Polyunsaturated Fat: 0 gm
Monounsaturated Fat: 0 gm

Cholesterol: 26 mg
Protein: 4 gm
Carbohydrate: 33 gm
Dietary Fiber: 1 gm
Sodium: 30 mg

Potato Cauliflower Kugel

Serves: 16

6 raw red potatoes, grated (~1 lb.)
1 head cauliflower, cooked and mashed
4 oz. grated onion
4 egg whites
1 tsp. low-sodium vegetable broth powder

1. Combine grated potatoes, mashed cauliflower, and grated onion.
2. Add beaten egg whites; mix well; add low-sodium vegetable broth powder.
3. Pour into pan, sprayed with non-stick cooking spray. Sprinkle with paprika.
4. Bake 30 minutes or until done in preheated oven at 350 degrees F.

Serving Size: 1 piece
Exchanges per Serving: ½ Starch, ½ Vegetable

Nutrition Facts

Calories: 42
Total Fat: 0 gm
Saturated Fat: 0 gm
Polyunsaturated Fat: 0 gm
Monounsaturated Fat: 0 gm

Cholesterol: 0 mg
Protein: 3 gm
Carbohydrate: 8 gm
Dietary Fiber: 1 gm
Sodium: 34 mg

Spinach Pie

Serves: 8

2 tsp. olive oil
2 lbs. fresh spinach or 2 (10 oz.) packages thawed frozen spinach
2 cups chopped scallions, including some green tops (~ 12)
1 cup matzoh meal
1 cup chopped fresh dill
8 egg whites
4 tbsp. lemon juice
2 whole matzoh
Salt and pepper to taste

1. Preheat oven to 350 degrees F. Spray the bottom and sides of a shallow 2 quart baking dish with non-stick cooking spray. Set aside.
2. Clean the fresh spinach, if using, removing the thick stems; chop coarsely (you will have about 8 cups).
3. Heat olive oil in a heavy skillet. Add the scallions and, after a couple of minutes, the spinach. Stir until wilted and well combined. Stir in the matzoh meal and combine well, using a wooden spoon. Add the dill. Remove the pan from the heat.
4. Beat the egg whites with the lemon juice until frothy, 4 or 5 minutes. Add the spinach mixture, salt, and pepper to taste.
5. Break the whole matzohs and scatter the pieces on the bottom of the sprayed pan. Pour the spinach mixture into the pan. Bake for 30-45 minutes, or until the top is nicely browned. Serve warm.

Serving Size: 1 slice
Exchanges per Serving: 1½ Starch, 1½ Vegetable, ½ Meat

Nutrition Facts

Calories: 157

Total Fat: 1.5 gm

Saturated Fat: 0 gm

Polyunsaturated Fat: 0 gm

Monounsaturated Fat: 1 gm

Cholesterol: 0 mg

Protein: 10 gm

Carbohydrate: 26 gm

Dietary Fiber: 3 gm

Sodium: 286 mg

Sweet Potato Kugel

Serves: 12

6 medium sweet potatoes, peeled and grated
3 small apples, peeled and grated
1 cup raisins
1 cup matzoh meal
2 tsp. cinnamon
1 cup water

1. Preheat oven to 375 degrees F.
2. Mix ingredients together. Press into large baking dish.
3. Bake 45 minutes until crisp on top.

Serving Size: 1 Piece
Exchanges per Serving: 1 ½ Starch, 1 Fruit

Nutrition Facts

Calories: 148
Total Fat: 0 gm
Saturated Fat: 0 gm
Polyunsaturated Fat: 0 gm
Monounsaturated Fat: 0 gm

Cholesterol: 0 mg
Protein: 2 gm
Carbohydrate: 35 gm
Dietary Fiber: 4 gm
Sodium: 38 mg

Vegetable Kugel

Serves: 8

6 zucchini, sliced
2 carrots, sliced
½ cup chopped onions
½ cup matzoh meal
1 tbsp. low-fat mayonnaise
1 whole egg
2 egg whites
1 tbsp. sugar
1 tsp. salt
½ tsp. pepper

1. Cook zucchini and carrots until soft. Drain and mash.
2. Combine with all other ingredients.
3. Pour into 9 inch pan, sprayed with non-stick cooking spray.
4. Sprinkle top lightly with matzo meal.
5. Bake at 375 degrees F for 1 hour.

Serving Size: 1 piece
Exchanges per Serving: 2 Vegetable, ½ Starch

Nutrition Facts

Calories: 87
Total Fat: 1 gm
Saturated Fat: 0 gm
Polyunsaturated Fat: 0 gm
Monounsaturated Fat: 0 gm

Cholesterol: 26 mg
Protein: 4 gm
Carbohydrate: 16 gm
Dietary Fiber: 2 gm
Sodium: 355 mg

Dairy Dishes

DAIRY DISHES

Broccoli Cheese Casserole

Serves: 8

4 ½ cups broccoli flowerets, parboiled
½ cup light sour cream
½ cup plain nonfat yogurt
1 cup nonfat cottage cheese
4 egg whites
1 cup hand cracked matzoh
1 large tomato, thinly sliced
4 tbsp. grated parmesan cheese

1. Preheat oven to 350 degrees F. Spray 11x 8 inch baking dish with non-stick cooking spray. Spread broccoli flowerets in dish.
2. In medium size mixing bowl, beat sour cream, yogurt, cottage cheese and egg whites until blended.
3. Fold in cracked matzoh and pour mixture over broccoli.
4. Arrange tomato slices on top and sprinkle with parmesan cheese. Bake in preheated oven for about 45 minutes.

Serving Size: 1 cup
Exchanges per Serving: 1 Meat, 1 ½ Vegetable, ½ Starch

Nutrition Facts

Calories: 111
Total Fat: 2.5 gm
Saturated Fat: 1.5 gm
Polyunsaturated Fat: 0 gm
Monounsaturated Fat: 0.5 gm

Cholesterol: 8 mg
Protein: 10 gm
Carbohydrate: 14 gm
Dietary Fiber: 3 gm
Sodium: 230 mg

Cottage Cheese Pancakes

Serves: 12

2 cups matzoh meal
¼ cup sugar
¾ lb. nonfat cottage cheese
1 egg
4 egg whites
1 ½ cups nonfat milk

1. Mix all ingredients into a very soft batter.
2. Form patties or drop batter by spoonfuls into a non-stick pan.
3. Brown on both sides and serve.

Serving Size: 2 pancakes
Exchanges per Serving: 1 ½ Starch, 1 Meat

Nutrition Facts

Calories: 130
Total Fat: 0 gm
Saturated Fat: 0 gm
Polyunsaturated Fat: 0 gm
Monounsaturated Fat: 0 gm

Cholesterol: 19 mg
Protein: 8 gm
Carbohydrate: 23 gm
Dietary Fiber: 1 gm
Sodium: 136 mg

Eggplant Lasagna

Serves: 6

1 tbsp. olive oil
3 cups sliced mushrooms
3 garlic cloves, crushed
¼ cup chopped fresh parsley
¼ cup dry red wine
1 tsp. dried basil
1 tsp. dried oregano
¼ tsp. crushed red pepper
¼ tsp. black pepper
1 (28 oz.) canned tomato puree
6 tbsp. grated Parmesan cheese
1 (15 oz.) container nonfat ricotta cheese
3 matzoh boards
1 large eggplant, peeled and sliced (~1 ¼ lbs.)

1. Heat oil in a saucepan over medium-high heat. Add mushrooms and garlic. Sauté for 5 minutes.
2. Stir in parsley, wine, basil, oregano, crushed red pepper, black pepper, and tomato puree. Partially cover and reduce heat to medium-low. Simmer for 30 minutes and then remove from heat.
3. Arrange eggplant slices in a single layer on baking sheet coated with cooking spray. Bake at 400 degrees F for 30 minutes, turning slices over after 15 minutes.
4. Remove from baking sheet and let cool. Cut eggplant slices into ½ inch pieces and set aside.
5. Combine ¼ cup Parmesan cheese and ricotta cheese in a bowl. Stir well and set aside.
6. Spread ½ cup tomato mixture in the bottom of an 11x7 inch baking dish coated with cooking spray. Arrange 1 ½ slices matzoh over tomato mixture and top with half ricotta cheese mixture, half of eggplant, and half of tomato mixture.
7. Repeat the layers, ending with the tomato mixture. Sprinkle with remaining 2 tbsp. of parmesan cheese.
8. Cover and bake at 350 degrees F for 45 minutes. Uncover and bake for an additional 15 minutes.

Serving Size: 1 serving
Exchanges per Serving: 1 Starch, 1 ½ Meat, 4 Vegetable, ½ Fat

□□□□□□□□□□□□□□□□□□□□

Nutrition Facts

Calories: 250
Total Fat: 7 gm
Saturated Fat: 3 gm
Polyunsaturated Fat: 0 gm
Monounsaturated Fat: 2 gm

Cholesterol: 22 mg
Protein: 12 gm
Carbohydrate: 33 gm
Dietary Fiber: 6 gm
Sodium: 632 mg

□□□□□□□□□□□□□□□□□□□□

Matzoh Brei Pancakes

Serves: 9

4 matzoh boards
¾ cup water
4 egg whites
2 egg yolks
Black pepper to taste
Curry powder to taste

1. Break matzoh into small pieces and place into a medium-size mixing bowl.
2. Add 1/3 cup water and stir. Let stand 2 minutes. Add remaining water, enough to just cover all matzoh pieces. Let stand 5 minutes.
3. Pour contents into a strainer and press out as much water as possible.
4. Beat egg whites, egg yolks and seasonings together. Stir in drained matzoh.
5. Spray a large non-stick skillet with non-stick cooking spray. Drop 2 tbsp. of matzoh mixture to make each pancake. Cook over medium-high heat for 2 minutes. Turn and cook an additional 1 minute or until golden brown.

Serving Size: 2 pancakes
Exchanges per Serving: 1 Starch

Nutrition Facts

Calories: 70
Total Fat: 1 gm
Saturated Fat: 0 gm
Polyunsaturated Fat: 0 gm
Monounsaturated Fat: 0 gm

Cholesterol: 47 mg
Protein: 4 gm
Carbohydrate: 11 gm
Dietary Fiber: 1 gm
Sodium: 27 mg

Matzoh Cheese Roll-Ups

Serves: 14

7 "prepared" matzohs
2 cups nonfat cottage cheese
2 egg whites
¼ cup reduced fat mozzarella cheese
1 garlic clove
Black pepper to taste
16 oz. marinara sauce
2 tbsp. parmesan cheese

1. Heat sauce.
2. In medium size mixing bowl, combine cottage cheese, egg whites, mozzarella cheese, garlic and black pepper; Mix well and set aside.
3. Cut matzoh in half and place one heaping tablespoon of cheese mixture on one end of matzoh and roll it up.
4. Place each stuffed matzoh onto 13x9x2 inch baking dish and cover with 2 cups of marinara sauce and parmesan cheese.
5. Bake in oven for 20 minutes at 400 degrees F.

Serving Size: 1 roll up
Exchanges per Serving: 1 Starch, 1 Meat, 1 Vegetable

Nutrition Facts

Calories: 114
Total Fat: 2 gm
Saturated Fat: 0.5 gm
Polyunsaturated Fat: 0 gm
Monounsaturated Fat: 0 gm

Cholesterol: 4 mg
Protein: 7 gm
Carbohydrate: 18 gm
Dietary Fiber: 1 gm
Sodium: 308 mg

Matzoh Meal Pancakes

Serves: 9

¾ cup matzoh meal
¾ tsp. salt
1 tbsp. sugar
¼ cup egg substitute
½ cup cold water or skim milk
4 egg whites

1. Combine the matzoh meal, salt, and sugar.
2. Beat the egg substitute lightly, add the water or milk, and combine with the matzoh meal mixture.
3. Beat the egg whites until stiff. Fold into the matzoh meal batter.
4. Spray a large, heavy skillet with non-stick cooking spray. Add batter by tablespoonfuls. Brown for 3 to 4 minutes, turn pancakes and brown for another 2 to 3 minutes. The pancakes should be golden on both sides. Serve immediately.

Serving Size: 2 pancakes
Exchanges per Serving: 1 Starch

Nutrition Facts

Calories: 86
Total Fat: 0 gm
Saturated Fat: 0 gm
Polyunsaturated Fat: 0 gm
Monounsaturated Fat: 0 gm

Cholesterol: 0 mg
Protein: 6 gm
Carbohydrate: 15 gm
Dietary Fiber: <1 gm
Sodium: 355 mg

Matzoh Pie

Serves: 10

8 medium potatoes
2 (10 oz.) packages frozen spinach, thawed and squeezed
5 scallions, diced
15 oz. fat free ricotta cheese
Juice of 1 lemon
Salt and pepper to taste
8 whole matzohs
1 cup part-skim mozzarella cheese, grated

1. Bake the potatoes in their skins until tender; cool. Peel and cut into ¼ inch thick slices.
2. Preheat oven to 350 degrees F.
3. In a mixing bowl, combine the spinach, scallions, ricotta cheese, lemon juice, salt and pepper.
4. Soak the matzohs in warm water in a shallow container until pliable but not mushy, about 2 minutes; drain.
5. Spray two 9x9 inch casserole dishes with non-stick spray; line the bottoms with a layer of matzohs. Layer each with the spinach mixture, potato slices, more matzohs and mozzarella cheese. Repeat until all ingredients are used. Finish with a layer of matzoh.
6. Bake until top matzoh is golden with spots of brown, about 25 to 30 minutes. Cut into squares to serve.

Serving Size: 1 piece
Exchanges per Serving: 2 ½ Starch, 2 Meat, ½ Vegetable

Nutrition Facts

Calories: 240
Total Fat: 1.5 gm
Saturated Fat: 1 gm
Polyunsaturated Fat: 0 gm
Monounsaturated Fat: 0 gm

Cholesterol: 16 mg
Protein: 12 gm
Carbohydrate: 43 gm
Dietary Fiber: 5 gm
Sodium: 487 mg

Potato Onion Pie

Serves: 10

3 onions, chopped
1 tbsp. olive oil
2 lbs. potatoes, just boiled and still warm
Salt
Black pepper, freshly ground
3 tbsp. potato starch
1 egg
4 egg whites
2 cups plain yogurt, nonfat
¼ cup parsley, minced

1. Preheat the oven to 350 degrees F. Spray a 10 inch pie plate with non-stick cooking spray.
2. Sauté the onions in the olive oil until softened and sweet, about 20 minutes.
3. While the onions cook, mash the still-warm potatoes with a potato masher or a fork. Add the potatoes to the onions, combining well. Add salt and pepper to taste.
4. Add the potato starch, stirring well to incorporate it completely. Add the eggs, egg whites, yogurt, and parsley.
5. Pour the mixture into the prepared pan and bake for 40 minutes, or until the top is lightly browned. Serve hot or at room temperature.

Serving Size: 1 piece
Exchanges per Serving: 1 ½ Starch, 1 Vegetable, ½ Milk

🔲🔲🔲🔲🔲🔲🔲🔲🔲🔲🔲🔲🔲🔲🔲🔲🔲🔲🔲🔲🔲

Nutrition Facts

Calories: 154
Total Fat: 2 gm
Saturated Fat: 0 gm
Polyunsaturated Fat: 0 gm
Monounsaturated Fat: 1 gm

Cholesterol: 22 mg
Protein: 7 gm
Carbohydrate: 27 gm
Dietary Fiber: 3 gm
Sodium: 307 mg

🔲🔲🔲🔲🔲🔲🔲🔲🔲🔲🔲🔲🔲🔲🔲🔲🔲🔲🔲🔲🔲

Raisin and Cheese Crepes

Serves: 8

Crepes
1 cup egg substitute
1 egg white
1/3 cup hot water
¼ cup potato starch
Pinch of salt

Filling
1 cup nonfat cottage cheese
½ cup raisins
½ tsp. cinnamon
Sweetener to taste

1. Beat egg substitute and egg white with salt and set aside.
2. Dissolve potato starch in hot water; mix well with beaten egg mixture.
3. Coat an 8 inch skillet with non-stick cooking spray.
4. Drop slightly less than ¼ cup into pan, spreading quickly to cover bottom of the pan. When golden, turn over. Repeat with rest of batter.
5. In a separate bowl, combine cottage cheese, raisins and cinnamon. If desired, add sweetener to taste.
6. Fill each crepe with 2 tbsp. cottage cheese mixture and fold together. Heat in oven until just warm.

Serving Size: 1 crepe with approximately 2 tbsp. filling
Exchanges per Serving: 1 Meat, ½ Starch, ½ Fruit

Nutrition Facts

Calories: 97
Total Fat: 1.5 gm
Saturated Fat: 0 gm
Polyunsaturated Fat: 0.5 gm
Monounsaturated Fat: 0 gm

Cholesterol: 2 mg
Protein: 8 gm
Carbohydrate: 13 gm
Dietary Fiber: 0 gm
Sodium: 215 mg

Sweet Matzoh Kugel

Serves: 16

12 "prepared" matzohs
10 egg whites
2/3 cup sugar
3 cups fat free milk
½ cup light sour cream
2 cups nonfat cottage cheese
1 ½ tsp. vanilla extract
1 cup raisins

1. Cut prepared matzoh into ½ inch strips. Set aside.
2. Beat egg whites well and thoroughly mix all the ingredients except for the prepared matzoh and raisins.
3. Fold in the matzoh and raisins.
4. Pour mixture into 9x13 inch glass baking dish, cover with plastic wrap and refrigerate overnight, or at least 3 hours to set consistency.
5. Preheat oven to 350 degrees F. Sprinkle top with cinnamon and bake 1 ½ hours or until golden brown.

Serving Size: 1 slice
Exchanges per Serving: 2 ½ Starch, 1 Meat, ½ Fruit

Nutrition Facts

Calories: 197
Total Fat: 1 gm
Saturated Fat: 0 gm
Polyunsaturated Fat: 0 gm
Monounsaturated Fat: 0 gm

Cholesterol: 4 mg
Protein: 10 gm
Carbohydrate: 39 gm
Dietary Fiber: 0 gm
Sodium: 166 mg

Tomato Cheese Matzoh Kugel

Serves: 6

4 matzoh boards, broken
3 ½ cups canned whole tomatoes, undrained
1 cup mushrooms, sliced
1 small onion, chopped
2 tsp. basil
2 tsp. oregano
Dash cayenne pepper, or to taste
2 egg whites
4 oz. of any kind of low-fat white or yellow cheese, shredded

1. Preheat oven to 375 degrees F.
2. In a bowl, combine the matzoh with the canned tomatoes and juice. Break up the tomatoes. Add the mushrooms, onion, basil, oregano, and cayenne pepper.
3. Beat the egg whites until stiff peaks form and fold into the matzoh mixture.
4. Coat a baking dish with the cooking spray and spoon the mixture into the dish. Bake for 35 minutes.
5. Spread the cheese over the top and bake for 10 minutes more, or until the cheese melts.

Serving Size: 1 cup
Exchanges per Serving: 1 ½ Starch, 1 Meat, 1 Vegetable

Nutrition Facts

Calories: 166
Total Fat: 3.5 gm
Saturated Fat: 1.5 gm
Polyunsaturated Fat: 0 gm
Monounsaturated Fat: 0 gm

Cholesterol: 7 mg
Protein: 10 gm
Carbohydrate: 24 gm
Dietary Fiber: 2 gm
Sodium: 457 mg

Desserts &
Baked Goods

DESSERTS &
BAKED GOODS

Apple Cake with Streusel Topping

Serves: 20

4 apples, peeled and sliced
4 tbsp. lemon juice
2 tsp. cinnamon
1 tsp. nutmeg
3 whole eggs
4 egg whites
1 cup sugar
1 tsp. vanilla extract
¼ cup oil
½ cup unsweetened applesauce
2 cups cake meal
2 tbsp. potato starch

Streusel Topping:
¼ cup sugar
1 ½ tsp. cinnamon
¼ cup chopped walnuts

1. Toss apples with lemon juice. Add cinnamon and nutmeg.
2. In a separate bowl, beat eggs and egg whites until fluffy, slowly adding sugar and vanilla extract.
3. Stir in oil, applesauce, cake meal, and potato starch. Pour half the batter into a 9x9 inch baking pan sprayed with non-stick cooking spray.
4. Spread apple mixture on top. Pour on the rest of the batter.
5. Combine streusel ingredients and sprinkle on top.
6. Bake in a preheated oven at 350 degrees F for one hour.

Serving Size: 1 slice
Exchanges per Serving: 1 Starch, 1 Fruit, 1 Fat

□□□□□□□□□□□□□□□□□□□□

Nutrition Facts

Calories: 178
Total Fat: 4.5 gm
Saturated Fat: 0 gm
Polyunsaturated Fat: 2.5 gm
Monounsaturated Fat: 1 gm

Cholesterol: 32 mg
Protein: 4 gm
Carbohydrate: 32 gm
Dietary Fiber: 1 gm
Sodium: 22 mg

□□□□□□□□□□□□□□□□□□□□

Apple Delight

Serves: 6

5 medium Granny Smith apples
¼ cup sugar
1 tsp. ground cinnamon
2 tsp. lemon juice

Topping:
½ cup matzoh meal
1/3 cup sugar
¼ cup almonds, sliced
1 tbsp. olive oil

1. Peel, core, and cut apples into ¼ inch slices.
2. Combine apple slices, sugar, cinnamon, and lemon juice. Toss gently. Spoon into an 11x7 inch baking dish coated with non-stick spray. Set aside.
3. For topping, combine matzoh meal, sugar, almonds, olive oil, and salt. Stir well. Sprinkle over apple mixture.
4. Bake at 350 degrees F for 1 hour or until browned.

Serving Size: 1 cup
Exchanges per Serving: 2 Fruit, 1 Starch, 1 Fat

Nutrition Facts

Calories: 221
Total Fat: 4 gm
Saturated Fat: 0 gm
Polyunsaturated Fat: 1 gm
Monounsaturated Fat: 3 gm

Cholesterol: 0 mg
Protein: 2 gm
Carbohydrate: 46 gm
Dietary Fiber: 4 gm
Sodium: 1 mg

NOTE: You can use sweetener in place of sugar. Calories will be 150 per serving with 27 grams of carbohydrate. Exchanges per Serving: 1 Fruit, 1 Starch, 1 Fat.

Apple Fritters

Serves: 14

2 medium apples
2 egg whites
4 tsp. potato starch
4 tbsp. hot water
½ tsp. cinnamon
Sweetener to taste

1. Grate apples and set aside.
2. Dissolve potato starch in hot water; combine with egg whites, cinnamon and sweetener. Fold in grated apple.
3. Drop by heaping teaspoonfuls into a pan coated with non-stick cooking spray. Brown on both sides.

Serving Size: 2 fritters
Exchanges per Serving: ½ Fruit

Nutrition Facts

Calories: 33
Total Fat: 0 gm
Saturated Fat: 0 gm
Polyunsaturated Fat: 0 gm
Monounsaturated Fat: 0 gm

Cholesterol: 0 mg
Protein: 1 gm
Carbohydrate: 8 gm
Dietary Fiber: 1 gm
Sodium: 16 mg

Banana Cake

Serves: 10

1 cup egg substitute
6 egg whites
2/3 cup sugar
1 tbsp. lemon juice
3 very ripe bananas, mashed
¼ tsp. salt
1 tsp. lemon zest
1 tsp. orange zest
¾ cup potato starch

1. Preheat oven to 350 degrees F. Spray a 10x3½ inch tube pan or 10 inch springform pan with non-stick cooking spray.
2. Beat the egg substitute, sugar, and lemon juice thoroughly, about 5 minutes.
3. Stir in the bananas, salt, lemon and orange zest. Sift in the potato starch. Beat for another minute.
4. In a separate bowl, beat the egg whites until they form soft peaks. Stir ¼ of the egg whites into the batter. Gently fold the rest of the egg whites into the batter.
5. Pour the mixture into the prepared pan. Bake for 30-40 minutes, or until a toothpick comes out clean and the top is nicely browned. Allow the cake to cool completely on a rack.

Serving Size: 1 piece
Exchanges per Serving: 1 ½ Starch, ½ Fruit

Nutrition Facts

Calories: 158
Total Fat: 1 gm
Saturated Fat: 0 gm
Polyunsaturated Fat: 0 gm
Monounsaturated Fat: 0 gm

Cholesterol: 0 mg
Protein: 6 gm
Carbohydrate: 33 gm
Dietary Fiber: 1 gm
Sodium: 136 mg

Basic Cookie

Serves: 30

2 cups cake meal
2 cups matzoh farfel
¾ cup sugar
1 tsp. ground cinnamon
½ cup oil
½ cup unsweetened applesauce
2 eggs, lightly beaten
4 egg whites, lightly beaten

1. Preheat oven to 350 degrees F.
2. Combine cake meal, farfel, sugar, cinnamon, oil, applesauce, eggs, and egg whites in a large bowl.
3. Using a tablespoon measure, form a ball with the dough and place onto baking sheet sprayed with non-stick cooking spray. Flatten cookies.
4. Bake for 20-30 minutes until golden brown.

Serving Size: 2 cookies
Exchanges per Serving: 1 Starch, 1 Fat

Nutrition Facts

Calories: 119
Total Fat: 4 gm
Saturated Fat: 0 gm
Polyunsaturated Fat: 3 gm
Monounsaturated Fat: 0.5 gm

Cholesterol: 14 mg
Protein: 3 gm
Carbohydrate: 18 gm
Dietary Fiber: 0 gm
Sodium: 12 mg

Brownie Bites

Serves: 24

2 eggs
4 egg whites
½ cup oil
1/3 cup unsweetened applesauce
1 cup sugar
½ cup cocoa
½ cup cake meal
1/3 cup potato starch

1. Beat eggs and egg whites together.
2. Add oil, applesauce and sugar and mix well.
3. Add remaining ingredients and blend together.
4. Pour into an 8x8 inch baking pan sprayed with non-stick cooking spray.
5. Bake at 350 degrees F for 30 minutes. When still warm, cut into small squares.

Serving Size: 1 piece
Exchanges per Serving: 1 Starch, 1 Fat

Nutrition Facts

Calories: 107
Total Fat: 5 gm
Saturated Fat: 0 gm
Polyunsaturated Fat: 3.5 gm
Monounsaturated Fat: 1 gm

Cholesterol: 18 mg
Protein: 2 gm
Carbohydrate: 14 gm
Dietary Fiber: 0 gm
Sodium: 18 mg

Cheesecake

Serves: 8

2 eggs, separated
½ cup sugar
½ cup lemon juice
1 lb. nonfat cottage cheese
1 cup skim milk
6 tbsp. matzoh meal
¼ tsp. salt

1. Beat egg yolks with sugar.
2. Combine lemon juice, cottage cheese, and milk and add alternately with matzoh meal to the egg and sugar mixture.
3. Beat egg whites with salt until stiff peaks form. Fold into the batter.
4. Bake at 325 degrees F for 1 hour in an 8 inch square pan. Turn off the oven and let the cake sit in the oven for another hour.

Serving Size: 1 slice
Exchanges per Serving: 1 Meat, 1 ½ Starch

Nutrition Facts

Calories: 146
Total Fat: 1.5 gm
Saturated Fat: 0 gm
Polyunsaturated Fat: 0 gm
Monounsaturated Fat: 0.5 gm

Cholesterol: 57 mg
Protein: 10 gm
Carbohydrate: 24 gm
Dietary Fiber: 0 gm
Sodium: 304 mg

Cheese Pudding

Serves: 6

1 ½ lb. nonfat cottage cheese
2 whole eggs, separated
4 egg whites
1 cup nonfat milk
1 tsp. lemon juice
1 tbsp. matzoh meal

1. Combine all ingredients except egg whites.
2. Beat egg whites until stiff.
3. Fold batter into whites.
4. Pour batter into a 2 quart casserole dish sprayed with non-stick cooking spray.
5. Bake at 300 degrees F for 1 hour. Turn off the oven and keep pudding in oven for 20-30 minutes.

Serving Size: ½ cup
Exchanges per Serving: 2 ½ Meat

□□□□□□□□□□□□□□□□□□□□□□

Nutrition Facts

Calories: 128
Total Fat: 2 gm
Saturated Fat: 0.5 gm
Polyunsaturated Fat: 0 gm
Monounsaturated Fat: 1 gm

Cholesterol: 67 mg
Protein: 18 gm
Carbohydrate: 10 gm
Dietary Fiber: 0 gm
Sodium: 470 mg

□□□□□□□□□□□□□□□□□□□□□□

Chocolate Cheesecake

Serves: 12

2 cups nonfat cottage cheese
8 oz. low fat cream cheese
2/3 cup granulated sugar
¼ cup cake meal
2 tbsp. unsweetened cocoa powder dissolved in ¼ cup boiling water
4 egg whites
1 tsp. vanilla extract

1. Preheat oven to 325 degrees F. Spray an 8 inch springform pan with non-stick cooking spray.
2. Prepare filling in food processor: puree cottage cheese and cream cheese, blend in sugar, cake meal, dissolved cocoa, egg whites and vanilla. Pour into pan.
3. Bake until set, approximately 1 hour. Turn oven off, prop open door and let cheesecake cool in oven for 1 hour. Cool completely on a rack.
4. Refrigerate in pan. Just before serving, unmold from pan and serve.

Serving Size: 1 slice
Exchanges per Serving: 1 Meat, 1 Starch, ½ Fat

Nutrition Facts

Calories: 125
Total Fat: 3.5 gm
Saturated Fat: 2 gm
Polyunsaturated Fat: 0 gm
Monounsaturated Fat: 1 gm

Cholesterol: 12 mg
Protein: 6 gm
Carbohydrate: 18 gm
Dietary Fiber: 0 gm
Sodium: 155 mg

Chocolate Chip Cookies

Serves: 18

1 egg
2 egg whites
½ cup sugar
½ cup oil
½ tsp. salt
1 cup matzoh meal
¼ cup cake meal
2 tbsp. potato starch
1 tsp. vanilla extract
¼ cup chocolate chips

1. Beat egg, egg whites, and sugar together.
2. Add oil, salt, matzoh meal, cake meal, potato starch and vanilla extract. Fold in chocolate chips.
3. Drop by teaspoon onto a cookie sheet sprayed with non-stick cooking spray.
4. Bake at 350 degrees F for 20-25 minutes.

Serving Size: 2 cookies
Exchanges per Serving: 1 Starch, 1 ½ Fat

Nutrition Facts

Calories: 130
Total Fat: 7 gm
Saturated Fat: 1 gm
Polyunsaturated Fat: 4.5 gm
Monounsaturated Fat: 1 gm

Cholesterol: 12 mg
Protein: 2 gm
Carbohydrate: 15 gm
Dietary Fiber: 0 gm
Sodium: 75 mg

Chocolate Chip Walnut Cookies

Serves: 24

1 cup matzoh meal
1 cup matzoh farfel
1/3 cup sugar
¼ cup chopped walnuts
2 tbsp. semisweet chocolate chips
1 egg
2 egg whites
1/3 cup oil

1. In a mixing bowl, combine matzoh meal, matzoh farfel, sugar, nuts and chocolate chips.
2. In a small bowl, beat egg and egg whites with oil.
3. Pour liquid mixture over dry ingredients. Mix until blended thoroughly.
4. Drop by teaspoonfuls, 2 inches apart, onto a baking sheet sprayed with non-stick cooking spray.
5. Bake in a preheated, 350 degree F oven for 20-30 minutes, or until golden.

Serving Size: 1 cookie
Exchanges per Serving: 1 Starch, 1 Fat

Nutrition Facts

Calories: 82
Total Fat: 4 gm
Saturated Fat: 0 gm
Polyunsaturated Fat: 2.5 gm
Monounsaturated Fat: 1 gm

Cholesterol: 9 mg
Protein: 2 gm
Carbohydrate: 9 gm
Dietary Fiber: 0 gm
Sodium: 8 mg

Cocoa Drops

Serves: 36

1 cup sugar
1 egg
2 egg whites
½ cup oil
½ cup applesauce
2 tsp. vanilla extract
2 tsp. baking powder
2 ½ cups cake meal
½ tsp. salt
½ cup cocoa

1. Combine the egg, egg whites and sugar and beat well.
2. Add the oil, applesauce and vanilla extract and mix.
3. Slowly add the remaining dry ingredients and mix thoroughly.
4. Drop by rounded teaspoonful onto a baking sheet sprayed with non-stick cooking spray. Bake at 350 degrees F for about 12-15 minutes.

Serving Size: 2 cocoa drops
Exchanges per Serving: 1 Starch, ½ Fat

Nutrition Facts

Calories: 97
Total Fat: 3 gm
Saturated Fat: 0 gm
Polyunsaturated Fat: 2 gm
Monounsaturated Fat: 0 gm

Cholesterol: 6 mg
Protein: 2 gm
Carbohydrate: 16 gm
Dietary Fiber: 0 gm
Sodium: 60 mg

Craisin Almond Macaroons

Serves: 16

½ cup sugar
4 tbsp. matzoh meal
6 egg whites
1 tsp. lemon juice
1 tsp. cinnamon
¼ tsp. ground ginger
1 cup craisins, chopped
1 cup whole almonds, ground in food processor

1. Preheat oven to 375 degrees F.
2. Make a mix of matzoh meal and 1 tbsp. sugar; set aside.
3. Beat egg whites until soft peaks form and add the remaining sugar. Beat until the consistency of marshmallow.
4. Add lemon juice, cinnamon, and ginger.
5. Gently fold in craisins and ground almonds.
6. Drop by teaspoonful onto cookie sheet sprayed with non-stick cooking spray. Sprinkle matzoh meal and sugar mixture over macaroons.
7. Bake 13-15 minutes.

Serving Size: 2 macaroons
Exchanges per Serving: 1 Starch, 1 Fat

Nutrition Facts

Calories: 115
Total Fat: 4.5 gm
Saturated Fat: 0 gm
Polyunsaturated Fat: 1 gm
Monounsaturated Fat: 3 gm

Cholesterol: 0 mg
Protein: 3 gm
Carbohydrate: 16 gm
Dietary Fiber: 2 gm
Sodium: 21 mg

Low Carb Cheesecake

Serves: 8

8 oz. Farmer cheese
2 egg whites
5 tsp. sugar
1 tsp. vanilla extract
1 tbsp. potato starch
2 tbsp. light sour cream
Cinnamon to taste

1. Place all ingredients in a blender except for cinnamon. Blend until well mixed and smooth.
2. Pour into pie plate, sprinkle cinnamon on top and bake at 350 degrees F for 20-25 minutes.

Serving Size: 1 slice
Exchanges per Serving: 1 Meat

Nutrition Facts

Calories: 72
Total Fat: 2.5 gm
Saturated Fat: 1.5 gm
Polyunsaturated Fat: 0 gm
Monounsaturated Fat: 0 gm

Cholesterol: 11 mg
Protein: 6 gm
Carbohydrate: 4 gm
Dietary Fiber: 0 gm
Sodium: 129 mg

Matzoh Meal Cookies

Serves: 21

2 eggs
2 egg whites
1/3 cup oil
¼ cup unsweetened applesauce
2/3 cup sugar
1 ¼ cups matzoh meal

1. Beat eggs, egg whites, oil, and applesauce together.
2. Add sugar and matzoh meal and mix well.
3. Drop by teaspoonful onto cookie sheet sprayed with non-stick cooking spray.
4. Bake for 20-25 minutes in a preheated 350 degree F oven.

Serving Size: 2 cookies
Exchanges per Serving: 1 Starch, 1 Fat

Nutrition Facts

Calories: 90
Total Fat: 3.5 gm
Saturated Fat: 0 gm
Polyunsaturated Fat: 2.5 gm
Monounsaturated Fat: 0.5 gm

Cholesterol: 20 mg
Protein: 2 gm
Carbohydrate: 13 gm
Dietary Fiber: 0 gm
Sodium: 12 mg

Matzoh Meal Mandelbrodt

Serves: 21

2 eggs
2 egg whites
1/3 cup oil
¼ cup unsweetened applesauce
2/3 cup sugar
1 ¼ cups matzoh meal
¼ tsp. cinnamon

1. Beat eggs, egg whites, oil, and applesauce together.
2. Add sugar and matzoh meal and mix well.
3. Shape dough into 2 loaves and place on a pan sprayed with non-stick cooking spray.
4. Bake for 20-25 minutes in a preheated 350 degree F oven.
5. Slice and add cinnamon on top. Return to oven for another 10 minutes.

Serving Size: 1 slice
Exchanges per Serving: 1 Starch, 1 Fat

Nutrition Facts

Calories: 90
Total Fat: 3.5 gm
Saturated Fat: 0 gm
Polyunsaturated Fat: 2.5 gm
Monounsaturated Fat: 0.5 gm

Cholesterol: 20 mg
Protein: 2 gm
Carbohydrate: 13 gm
Dietary Fiber: 0 gm
Sodium: 12 mg

Muffins

Serves: 12

1 ½ cups boiling water
2 tbsp. sugar
1 tsp. salt
2 cups matzoh meal
2 eggs
4 egg whites
1/3 cup oil

1. Dissolve sugar and salt in the boiling water.
2. Pour sugar and salt solution over matzoh meal and mix well. Let stand 5 minutes.
3. Beat eggs and egg whites with a fork and add oil. Add to matzoh meal mixture.
4. Pour mixture into muffin pan sprayed with non-stick cooking spray.
5. Bake at 350 degrees F for 50-60 minutes.

Serving Size: 1 muffin
Exchanges per Serving: 1 ½ Starch, 1 Fat

Nutrition Facts

Calories: 152
Total Fat: 7 gm
Saturated Fat: 0.5 gm
Polyunsaturated Fat: 2 gm
Monounsaturated Fat: 4 gm

Cholesterol: 35 mg
Protein: 4 gm
Carbohydrate: 18 gm
Dietary Fiber: 1 gm
Sodium: 225 mg

Orange Cake

Serves: 24

2 eggs
2 egg whites
¾ cup sugar
½ cup oil
1 tbsp. baking powder
2 cups orange juice
2 cups cake meal
2 tsp. vanilla extract

1. Beat eggs and egg whites with sugar. Add oil and mix.
2. Add baking powder, orange juice, cake meal, and vanilla extract. Beat for a few minutes.
3. Pour batter into a 9x13 inch baking pan coated with non-stick cooking spray.
4. Bake for 40-50 minutes in a preheated 350 degrees F oven.

Serving Size: 1 piece
Exchanges per Serving: 1½ Starch, 1 Fat

□ □ □ □ □ □ □ □ □ □ □ □ □ □ □ □ □ □ □

Nutrition Facts

Calories: 132
Total Fat: 5 gm
Saturated Fat: 0 gm
Polyunsaturated Fat: 3.5 gm
Monounsaturated Fat: 1 gm

Cholesterol: 18 mg
Protein: 2 gm
Carbohydrate: 20 gm
Dietary Fiber: 0 gm
Sodium: 56 mg

□ □ □ □ □ □ □ □ □ □ □ □ □ □ □ □ □ □ □

Pie Crust

Serves: 8

1 cup matzoh meal
3 tbsp. oil
1 tbsp. water
2 tbsp. sugar
½ tsp. salt
¼ tsp. cinnamon

1. Blend all ingredients together.
2. Press into a 9 inch pie plate. Bake at 375 degrees F for 15-20 minutes, until golden brown.
3. Cool and fill with desired filling.

Serving Size: 1/8 pie crust
Exchanges per Serving: 1 Starch, 1 Fat

Nutrition Facts

Calories: 112
Total Fat: 5 gm
Saturated Fat: 0 gm
Polyunsaturated Fat: 4 gm
Monounsaturated Fat: 0.5 gm

Cholesterol: 0 mg
Protein: 2 gm
Carbohydrate: 15 gm
Dietary Fiber: <1 gm
Sodium: 146 mg

Pineapple-Cherry Ribbon

Serves: 32

8 cups crushed pineapple, canned in juice
1 (0.33 oz) packet diet cherry jello mix
8 cups hot water
4 cups fat free vanilla ice cream

1. Drain pineapple, reserving the liquid.
2. Place ½ packet jello mix into mixing bowl. Add hot water and stir until dissolved.
3. Blend in drained pineapple.
4. Pour mixture into a 12 x 17 x 2 inch pan and refrigerate until set.
5. Add water to reserved pineapple liquid to measure 4 cups. Heat to 140-160 degrees F.
6. Add hot liquid to remaining jello mix. Stir until dissolved.
7. Add ice cream. Stir until ice cream is melted and mixture is thoroughly blended.
8. Pour ice cream mixture over pineapple layer in pan. Cover and refrigerate until firm.
9. Cut into 8 by 4 inch pieces for suggested Serving Size.

Serving Size: 1 piece
Exchanges per Serving: ½ Fruit, ½ Milk

Nutrition Facts

Calories: 61
Total Fat: 0 gm
Saturated Fat: 0 gm
Polyunsaturated Fat: 0 gm
Monounsaturated Fat: 0 gm

Cholesterol: 0 mg
Protein: 1 gm
Carbohydrate: 14 gm
Dietary Fiber: 1 gm
Sodium: 40 mg

Rolls

Serves: 12

1 cup boiling water
¼ cup olive oil
1 ¼ cup matzoh meal
¾ cup egg substitue
2 egg whites
1 tbsp. sugar

1. Combine boiling water with oil in a pot; bring to a boil.
2. Lower heat and add matzoh meal; remove from heat, stirring quickly until mixture forms a ball.
3. Add egg substitute, then add egg whites one at a time, stirring continuously.
4. Add sugar and mix; dough should be smooth and thick.
5. Drop by tablespoonfuls onto baking sheet sprayed with non-stick cooking spray.
6. Bake in preheated 400 degree F oven for 40 minutes, until golden.

Serving Size: 1 roll
Exchanges per Serving: 1 Starch, 1 Fat

Nutrition Facts

Calories: 114
Total Fat: 5 gm
Saturated Fat: 1 gm
Polyunsaturated Fat: 1 gm
Monounsaturated Fat: 3.5 gm

Cholesterol: 0 mg
Protein: 4 gm
Carbohydrate: 13 gm
Dietary Fiber: 0 gm
Sodium: 38 mg

Scrumptious Chocolate Cake

Serves: 30

1 ½ cups sugar
½ cup oil
1 ½ cups unsweetened applesauce
2 cups egg substitute
4 egg whites
2 tsp. vanilla extract
1 cup cocoa
¾ cup matzoh meal
½ cup potato starch
1 tsp. baking powder
1 tsp. baking soda

1. Beat sugar and oil together.
2. Add remaining ingredients and mix well. Pour batter into a 9x13 inch pan sprayed with non-stick cooking spray.
3. Bake at 350 degrees F for approximately 1 hour.

Serving Size: 1 piece
Exchanges per Serving: 1 Starch, 1 Fat

Nutrition Facts

Calories: 119
Total Fat: 4 gm
Saturated Fat: 0 gm
Polyunsaturated Fat: 3 gm
Monounsaturated Fat: 0.5 gm

Cholesterol: 0 mg
Protein: 3 gm
Carbohydrate: 17 gm
Dietary Fiber: 0 gm
Sodium: 96 mg

Soft and Chewy Cinnamon Mandelbrodt

Serves: 16

1/3 cup oil
¼ cup unsweetened applesauce
2/3 cup sugar
¾ cup egg substitute
2 egg whites
1 ½ cups cake meal
6 tbsp. potato starch
1 tsp. salt
2 tsp. lemon juice

1. Mix all ingredients in a bowl.
2. Form into 2 large rolls.
3. Bake for 30 minutes at 350 degrees F until brown.
4. Cut into slices and turn slices onto side and sprinkle with a small amount of cinnamon and sugar.
5. Bake for another 5 minutes.

Serving Size: 1 slice
Exchanges per Serving: 1½ Starch, 1 Fat

Nutrition Facts

Calories: 157
Total Fat: 5 gm
Saturated Fat: 0 gm
Polyunsaturated Fat: 3.5 gm
Monounsaturated Fat: 1 gm

Cholesterol: 0 mg
Protein: 3 gm
Carbohydrate: 25 gm
Dietary Fiber: 0 gm
Sodium: 173 mg

Sponge Cake

Serves: 12

½ cup egg substitute
2 eggs
2 egg whites
¼ cup hot water
¾ cup sugar
1 tsp. vanilla extract
1 cup cake meal

1. Beat egg substitute, eggs, and eggs whites well.
2. Pour hot water over sugar to melt and allow to cool. Add to egg mixture.
3. Add vanilla extract and cake meal.
4. Pour into an 8 x 8 inch pan sprayed with non-stick cooking spray and bake at 350 degrees F for 20 minutes.

Serving Size: 1 piece
Exchanges per Serving: 1½ starch

□□□□□□□□□□□□□□□□□□□□□□

Nutrition Facts

Calories: 123
Total Fat: 1 gm
Saturated Fat: 0 gm
Polyunsaturated Fat: 0 gm
Monounsaturated Fat: 0 gm

Cholesterol: 35 mg
Protein: 4 gm
Carbohydrate: 24 gm
Dietary Fiber: 0 gm
Sodium: 39 mg

□□□□□□□□□□□□□□□□□□□□□□

APPENDIX A

<u>Measurement Equivalents</u>

1 ½ teaspoons	= ½ tablespoon
3 teaspoons	= 1 tablespoon
2 tablespoons	= 1/8 cup
4 tablespoons	= ¼ cup
5 1/3 tablespoons	= 1/3 cup
8 tablespoons	= ½ cup
10 2/3 tablespoons	= 2/3 cup
16 tablespoons	= 1 cup
¼ pound	= 4 ounces
½ pound	= 8 ounces
¾ pound	= 12 ounces
1 pound	= 16 ounces
1 tablespoon	= ½ fluid ounce
2 tablespoons	= 1 fluid ounce
1 cup	= 8 fluid ounces
2 cups	= 1 pint
4 cups	= 1 quart
2 pints	= 1 quart
1 quart	= 32 ounces
4 quarts	= 1 gallon
1 peck	= 8 quarts
1 bushel	= 4 pecks

<u>Metric Conversions</u>

1 ounce	= 28.35 grams
1 pound	= 453.59 grams
1 gram	= 0.035 ounces
1 kilogram	= 2.2 pounds
1 teaspoon	= 4.9 milliliters
1 tablespoon	= 14.79 milliliters
1 cup	= 236.6 milliliters
1 quart	= 946.4 milliliters
1 liter	= 1.06 quarts

APPENDIX B

Tips for Sodium Reduction

At the supermarket...

- Be a label reader. Look for information on sodium content of foods and learn to recognize high-sodium ingredients.

- When shopping for low-sodium foods, fresh is usually best. Fresh fruits, vegetables, meats, and unprocessed grains are generally low in sodium. Most convenience foods are high in sodium, so limit your intake of prepared foods.

- Consider low and reduced-sodium products. If you must severely restrict your sodium intake, you can buy low-sodium breads, cheeses, crackers, cereals, soups, baking powder, margarine, snack foods, condiments, processed meats, and other products. Shop carefully because such products can be expensive and the labels can be misleading. It might prove more economical to prepare your own low-sodium versions at home.

In the kitchen...

- Plan meals that contain less sodium. Consult low-sodium cookbooks, and try new recipes that limit the salt and sodium-containing ingredients.

- Adjust your recipes by reducing the salty ingredients a little at a time. Don't be fooled by recipes without added table salt that call for soups, bouillon cubes, or condiments high in salt!

- In many recipes, you can omit salt without losing much flavor. However, in baking, especially with yeast, salt may be required to control fermentation. You can experiment to see what works.

- Don't add salt in cooking pasta, rice, noodles, hot cereals, or vegetables.

- Experiment with herbs, spices, and other seasonings as alternatives to high-sodium condiments. Try onion, garlic, vinegar, lemon juice or lemon zest, freshly grated horseradish, pepper, small amounts of sugar, or dry wines to add flavor to foods.

- Avoid canned foods whenever possible. Alternatively, rinse canned foods containing sodium under running water for one minute. About one-third to one-half of the sodium can be washed out of canned vegetables and canned tuna using this simple technique.

- Foods you prepare yourself can contain significantly less sodium than commercially prepared products. When you make food from scratch *you* control how much sodium is added.

At the table...

- Taste your foods before you salt it. If, after tasting, you want to add salt, try one quick shake instead of being heavy handed.

- Limit the amount of condiments you add to your food, or try the low-sodium products.

- Moderate your selection of high-sodium foods. In some instances, all you need to do is cut down, not cut out! It's the total amount of sodium in your diet that counts. Check with your doctor regarding the type of sodium restriction you need and follow doctors' orders.

APPENDIX C

<u>Cooking and Baking Substitutions</u>

Instead of...	Use...
Milk, whole	Fat free or 1% milk
Eggs	2 egg whites or ¼ cup egg substitute per egg
Chocolate chips	Dried fruit
Nuts	½ the required amount toasted to increase flavor
Cream	Equal parts 1% milk and fat free evaporated milk
Sour cream	Light sour cream or fat free plain yogurt
Butter	Low fat margarine or oil
Fruit-flavored yogurt	Fat-free plain yogurt mixed with fresh or frozen fruit
Whipping cream	Fat-free whipped topping or evaporated skim milk (chilled)
Syrup	Sugar-free syrup, sugar-free preserves or pureed fruit

Instead of...	Use...
Coconut	1/2 amount required, toasted to enhance flavor
Fruit canned in syrup	Fruit canned in water or juices
Mayonnaise	Reduced-fat or fat-free versions, low-fat or fat-free plain yogurt
Oil (in baking)	Equal amounts of applesauce

APPENDIX D

Food Labeling Terms

Term	Definition
Low Calorie	40 calories or less per serving.
Cholesterol Free	Less than 2 milligrams cholesterol and 2 grams or less saturated fat per serving.
Low Cholesterol	20 milligrams or less cholesterol and 2 grams or less saturated fat per serving.
Saturated Fat Free	Less than 0.5 gram saturated fat per serving and the level of trans fatty acids does not exceed 1% of total fat.
Low Saturated Fat	1 gram or less saturated fat per serving and not more than 15% of calories from saturated fat.
Fat Free	Less than 0.5 gram fat per serving and does not contain added ingredients that are fats.
Low Fat	3 grams or less fat per serving.
Salt Free or Sodium Free	Less than 5 milligrams sodium per serving and does not contain sodium chloride (table salt).

Term	Definition
Very Low Sodium	35 milligrams or less sodium per serving.
Low Sodium	140 milligrams or less sodium per serving.
Lean	Meat, poultry and seafood with less than 10 grams fat, less than 4.5 grams saturated fat, and less than 95 milligrams cholesterol per serving and per 100 grams.
Extra Lean	Meat, poultry and seafood with less than 5 grams fat, less than 2 grams saturated fat, and less than 95 milligrams cholesterol per serving and per 100 grams.
Good Source of....	10-19% of the Daily Value for a particular nutrient per serving.
High in...	20% or more of the Daily Value for a particular nutrient per serving.
Light or Lite	Either (1) The food contains 1/3 fewer calories or 50% less fat than the higher-calorie, higher-fat version; so if the food derives 50% or more of its calories from fat, the reduction must be 50% of the fat, or (2) The sodium content of a low-calorie, low-fat food has been reduced by 50%.

Term	Definition
	Note: *the term "light" still can be used to describe such properties as texture and color, as long as the label/packaging explains the intent.*
Reduced	A nutritionally-altered food that contains at least 25% less of a nutrient than a reference food.
Less	A food, whether altered or not, which contains 25% less of a nutrient or of calories than the reference food.
Healthy	A food that is low in fat and saturated fat, contains 480 milligrams or less sodium, limited amounts of cholesterol and provides at least 10% of the Daily Value for one or more of these nutrients: vitamin A, vitamin C, iron, calcium, protein, and fiber.

A "Serving" is a reference amount of more than 30 grams or more than 2 tablespoons. Different criteria may apply for smaller reference amounts.

INDEX OF RECIPES

Kugels..83

Dairy Dishes 97

Desserts & Baked Goods 111

Breinigsville, PA USA
25 March 2011
258478BV00001B/5/P